THE
TAROT
ALMANAC

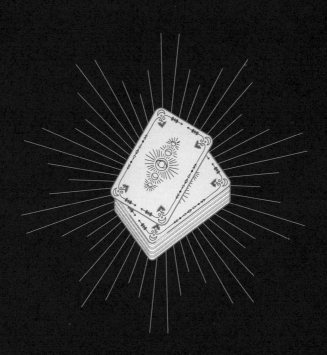

THE
TAROT
ALMANAC

A Seasonal Guide
to Divining with
Your Cards

◇

BESS MATASSA

STERLING ETHOS
New York

STERLING ETHOS
New York

ISBN 978-1-4549-4783-7

Library of Congress Control Number: 2022951040

For information about custom editions, special sales, and premium purchases, please contact
specialsales@unionsquareandco.com.

Printed in China

2 4 6 8 10 9 7 5 3 1

unionsquareandco.com

Cover design by Gina Bonanno
Endpapers and interior design by Gina Bonanno

Picture credits appear on p. 265

To all of my mystical mentors
and covenettes—especially
Lanie Kagan and Lindsay Mack

CONTENTS

INTRODUCTION

All of life lies beneath your fingertips, waiting to be turned over. If you've touched it, tasted it, sniffed it—if you've loved it, lost it, lived through it, then learned to love it all over again: there is absolutely a tarot card for it. Every single sensation, experience, and way of being human can find a home within the borders of one of these seventy-eight heart-shaped locket life-worlds. Already alive and well within you and just longing for your tender touch, the tarot is innately yours. And it's yours to play for keeps.

Our own lives are speaking to us through symbols all the time. From the teensiest ladybug sidestepping across your dashboard, sporting a secret message for you on its winged back; to the thumping bassline of a pop song overheard at a stoplight that just won't quit until you've felt it fully—the tarot is yet another love note in the world's chatty cosmic chorus, forever buzzing with customized communiqués. One divinely inspired dialect among many, we can use the tarot to help translate what we're up to and why we're here. This magic tool gives us poetic power and the prowess to take a ride on this tilt-a-whirlwind we call life, no matter where it may lead us.

When we pull a card from the deck, we can consciously choose to dance with the divinity that exists within each of us and invisibly surrounds us in every moment. We can lift our lives high above our heads like pairs of figure skaters and spin the sparkling details of each moment into valuable insight. Turning over each card is a chance to see our life stories as operatic dramas, full of exhilarating soul growth. It takes courage, muscle, and plenty of tassels to live the tarot this way. But we have only one shot at living in these beautiful bods, so we had better make it epic.

Think of your tarot deck as your first technicolor trip to the cinema: a pair of slip-on glasses that take you out of black-and-white silent films and straight into

Hollywood's golden era. The tarot is an ice-cream parlor, stocked with absolutely every flavor available for savoring—from delicate rosewater that dilates the taste buds in cool sweetness, all the way to the thick palate-coating carnality of rich chili chocolate. A prismatic psychic hotline leading straight to your own soul, your deck both reflects and refracts the stuff of your already-vital existence through its seventy-eight sensations.

The briny maritime mists of the Moon card, beckoning you out after dark for a skinny-dip into your deep end. The panoramic picnic basket vistas of the King of Swords, urging you to bear witness to the width of your inner weather with wonderment. The pulse-point peony perfume of the Six of Cups, insisting that yes, there is life after love; and yes, there is still love to be had within it. Each card is a chance to explore a different "archetype"—a symbol that speaks to a shared part of our human experience. Taken in its entirety, our deck offers a full-spectrum echo of what life already does best: dip us in every last stripe of the emotional rainbow in service of our evolution.

Your deck doesn't foretell future perfects or portend ominous omens. It doesn't magically solve algebraic equations, fill holes in your heart, or regrout the bathroom tile. Instead, it speaks up from within you, *for* you. Translating love notes on behalf of bits of your beingness that you can't always bring yourself to speak into being just yet. Little soul whispers that meet you outside your window after midnight with a care package, urging you onward when you think all is lost. Clarion calls served up like cinnamon atop your caffe latte at daybreak, invigorating you toward inevitable life change. You can call these communiqués god. Or the divine. Or the unseen world. Or you can just call them another part of your own sweet self, beaming at you from a parallel meridian that wants to honeymoon you into the grand romance of your next incarnation.

We can certainly do all this living and loving and learning without the tarot. But with it, we're gifted a veritable Vegas buffet of beingness. And with nothing to lose and our most vivid, vital selves to gain, we lay all our cards on the table—settling in for an all-you-can-eat feast fashioned from seventy-eight flavors and then some.

HOW TO USE THIS BOOK

Everything is alive, and you are part of it. Breathing. Colliding. Exchanging. Changing. Each season, roses burst into riotous bloom and then loosen their petals to power the compost of this never-ending story all over again. And in turn, these cycles here on earth are set to the soundtrack of the stars—also known as astrology. By aligning tarot to these stellar shifts, this book beckons you to breathe in and out along with the Universe itself.

For as long as humans have existed, we've been looking skyward for meaning and mythos. With roots thousands of years back in Babylon and beyond, astrology is an interpretive art that tracks planetary movements in support of emotional evolution down here on the ground. And whatever tarot's ultimate lineage—some say it has ancient Egyptian beginnings in addition to its more obvious link to fifteenth-century packs of playing cards—all of tarot's archetypes reverberate with astrology's essence. Each of the seventy-eight cards carries a piece of the cosmos in its DNA through its symbolic association with one of the astrological signs, planets, elements, or a combination thereof.

During each month on planet earth, the energies shift in the heavens, creating collective "feeling tones" that we all experience. As the sun moves through one of the twelve stripes of the sky watched over by one of the twelve zodiac signs, we call this an astrological season. And as we travel through that month's astro season, a family of tarot cards steps forward to support the shooting-star show. Take July, for example, with its languid, self-contained quality, as private and purse-like as a seashell. This month is led by Cancer energy in astrology. As the sun Slip 'N Slides through this watery zodiac sign's forcefield, the symbolic shift invites all of us (regardless of our particular "sign") to tuck in toward tenderness, incubating our wildest dreams. In turn, each card in the tarot is infused with an astrological "charge" that can be related to one of the twelve zodiac signs. So, in this book, July's landscape is covered by Cancerian cuties the High Priestess, the Chariot, and the Ace, 2, 3, and 4 of Cups—all invitations to consider our inner sanctuaries, innate lovability, and capacity to caretake ourselves as we ebb and flow with life's sea-soaked emotional shifts.

When we touch in with the tarot in this way, we find resonance between what lives inside of us and everything that surrounds us. We vibrate to the hum of this whole world, and begin to experience an energetic duet with the very seasons of our lives.

◆ Note that because the astrological and Gregorian calendars aren't perfectly synced, an astro season doesn't last the full month, and the start date of each season shifts slightly from year to year (so, for example, Leo season, which follows after Cancer, technically starts sometime in late July, but might not occur on exactly the same date every year). But because we enter and spend the bulk of a given month balleting through that sign's energy before we flip into the next, near month's end, we'll chart our course through the cards accordingly.

Author's Note

The tarot is not just a deck of seventy-eight cards: it is a vivid, living language that can help us awaken our deepest evolutionary potentials, rainbowed hopes, and roll-the-dice dreams. That said, this content is intended for entertainment purposes only (ah, the amusement park of our consciousness!), and is not here to take the place of any type of medical advice or formal therapeutic practice. Snuggle up to the suggestions that feel closest to your heart and toss the rest out the wide-open window of your psyche's convertible. I am a person. You are a person. And *you* are always the ultimate expert in divining your own intuitive experience. Let's play!

Structuring Your Monthly Practice

....

Your tarot deck is divided into three card categories: the Major Arcana (twenty-one cards, plus the Fool); the Minor Arcana (four suits of ten cards each); and the Court cards (four suits of four cards each). Each month's treasure chest will include cards from each category. You're always welcome to freeform your engagement with these card categories each month, bopping between their teachings according to your own intuitive rhythm. Or, if you fancy a more finite timeline, you can follow the tri-part practice outlined below:

⟩MONTH'S DEBUT⟨
(WEEKS 1–2)

The Major Arcana are our *soul biospheres*: they beckon us to breathe into the big old shifts and embrace epic evolutionary themes, wilding through the weather of a season in our lives that wants to steep us in its teachings. The Major Arcana sections introduce you to the key emotional invitations for that month.

You can think of the Major Arcana cards the same way you would physical landscapes, taking the start of the month to land within them and orient yourself to their energetic environments. Accordingly, parts of their descriptions are more experiential: intended to invite you to step inside of them and take a look around, observing their themes without having to cling too tightly to prescriptive meanings.

During the first few weeks of the month, let yourself play with entering these card countries. You might do this by simply reading the description and then closing your eyes and letting it wash over you—imagining yourself wading into the world it describes and seeing what images come up. Or, you might use artwork from your own deck to complement the process, gazing at the card meditatively and picturing yourself entering the scene that's depicted and seeing how it feels to live within it. You can even seek out actual environments that feel symbolically connected (i.e. choosing a seat on a train's quiet car or burrowing into the back of your closet to commune with the High Priestess card in July). There are a few "turf tips" listed for each of the Majors to help inspire your wanderings.

You can also use the Majors to root you in a **daily practice** by returning to their key questions. See how these inquiries might evolve for you in each magic moment of the month by checking in with them first thing in the morning or at the end of each day. If you'd like extra support, you can always pull another card from your deck to help you answer them (this practice can, of course, be employed at any time during the year for any of the self-inquiry questions in this book).

⟫MID-MONTH⟪
(WEEKS 2–3)

The Minor Arcana are *today's specials*: the sandwich boards that serve up lessons for life on the ground, these cards ask us to taste the treats of the moment and take action in tangible ways. The Minor Arcana sections of each month are here to spark immediate application and provide down-to-earth "to-dos" for living the tarot.

You can let your engagement with the Minors form the centerpiece of each month as you dig into the nitty-gritty of magical work. During this mid-month practice, you might gather the three to four cards listed and draw one each day—spending that day really living and breathing its energies by heeding its teachings through direct action, and noticing how its themes show up in your emotions, endeavors, and encounters with others.

⟫MONTH'S CLOSE⟪
(WEEKS 3–4)

The Court Cards are our *body suits*: like frocks hanging in our closets, these slip-on sweeties are here to escort us back into essential ways of being, reconnecting us with—and activating—parts of our identities. The Court Card sections of each month offer advice on how to embody these subtle energies.

There are as many ways to "be" each of the Court Cards as there are human beings (i.e. there's no right way to embody Queen of Wands energy, and there's not one kind of person who's more adept at it than another). Each month includes a "style quiz" to help you explore how you can express that card's archetype in a way that best fits you. Toward each month's close, you can think of the Court Cards as your graduation from all the themes you've been working with over the previous weeks. Use this time to practice walking their walk and living their essence as you prepare to advance from one month to the next.

Additionally, in each month's chapter you'll find a **card spread** and **"magic trick"** tip to help you deepen your tarot practice and connect more intimately with your deck, inspired by that month's energies. Each spread sketches some contours for questioning and is intended to be adaptable; you can tailor it to whatever life situation you might find yourself wandering through in that moment—asking about anything from an upcoming work presentation, to your quest for true love, to what kind of meal might taste most delicious for lunch. There is no inquiry that's too esoteric or too mundane. Trust that you'll know what's in need of more clarity; and that whatever way you pose your questions will be exactly right. Just like any close confidante, the tarot just wants to dialogue with you. Pose your questions in the same way you would to a friend.

In each month's cosmic kit, you'll also find a **tarotscopes** section, which showcases one of that month's cards that can help give your sign an extra lift and squeeze as you travel.

As the sun travels through a new zodiac sign each month, we each experience the terrain slightly differently, according to our own astrology. You can work with each month's scope for your sign in any way that you choose: magnetizing it to your fridge as a reminder note; sitting down to muse on its imagery; or even pulling other cards from your deck to help you activate its invitations, asking how you might open to even more of its treats.

You can start simply, by reading the scope for your Sun sign (aka your "zodiac sign" or "star sign" if you're fresh to the astro block). If you're feeling extra fancy, you can also read the scopes for your Moon and/or Rising signs. Our Sun sign marks us with our very own superhero mission of individual expression. The Moon connects us to the seashell-abratory emotional currents of our inner world. And our Rising offers up a rendezvous with the epic adventure of it all: asking us to open the door to the experiences that long to lead and shape us. Pick whatever your passion (or all three!), and take a plunge.

The Three Qualities

....

Each month's flavor is imbued with a rhythmic charge, which moves and grooves it in a given direction. Through each of the three months within the four seasons, we can align ourselves with this bump 'n' grind, noticing how things begin (Cardinal energy); how they endure (Fixed energy); and how they fall away (Mutable energy).

⇒ CARDINAL ⇐

STARTING LINE SPARK PLUGS. Kicking off each of the year's four seasons, this energy turns all of existence on—powering up, pointing the way, and asking us to consider the impact of life's forces.

(Capricorn, Aries, Cancer, and Libra energy in
January, April, July, and October)

⇒ FIXED ⇐

HAVE-AND-HOLD HOTHOUSES. Securing us in the centerpiece of the four seasons, this energy steeps us in its treats—plus-sizing us into greater presence and stabilizing our storehouses of inner strength.

(Aquarius, Taurus, Leo, and Scorpio energy in
February, May, August, and November)

⇒ MUTABLE ⇐

MOOD RING MEDIUMS. Confetti-tossing us toward the four seasons' finales in wild style, this energy invites us to let it all pass through—respirating, releasing, and chameleoning across thresholds.

(Pisces, Gemini, Virgo, and Sagittarius energy in
March, June, September, and December)

The Four Elements

....

If you ever feel lost or unmoored as you start to wile your way through the seventy-eight cards of the tarot in each of the twelve months of the year, you can summon the simple superpower of the four elements. Each of the twelve astrological signs is made from the stuff of one of these elements, and, in turn, each of the tarot cards you'll encounter contains an elemental essence. This quartet's meanings are matter of fact, and their matter can be found absolutely anywhere; to experience their energies, simply start by looking around your immediate physical environment for evidence of their presence.

⋟ FIRE ⋞

IMMORTALIZING. This is the realm of fundamental aliveness, self-expression, and larger-than-life meaning making. Light a burner on the stove and crack an egg, feeling the fresh-and-ready breakfast initiation sensations of Fire's fry-'em-up flair.

(Aries, Leo, and Sagittarius energy in April, August, and December)

⋟ EARTH ⋞

FORTIFYING. This is the realm of embodiment, tangible resources, and ritualized rhythms. Settle down into your leather lounger and back into the seat of your soul for some farm-to-table snacking on Earth's worldly worthiness.

(Capricorn, Taurus, and Virgo energy in January, May, and September)

⚛ AIR ⚛

CLARIFYING. This is the realm of aspiration, reflection, and consciousness shifts. Slide the porch doors open and adjust the Venetian blinds toward Air's color-changing, circulatory spaciousness.

(Aquarius, Gemini, and Libra energy in February, June, and October)

⚛ WATER ⚛

SENSITIZING. This is the realm of intimacy, fusion, and emotional pulls. Fill the tub with sudsy scented bath bubbles and slip out of your fuzzy robe and into Water's private pool plunge.

(Pisces, Cancer, and Scorpio energy in March, July, and November)

Let these four basic beauty building blocks be your foundation as you explore the wider world, uncovering different expressions of these elements all around you.

The Twelve Months

....

Use the crib sheet below to start feeling into the stardust that's getting served up each month.

JANUARY: THE MAGIC OF GRAVITY

A bone-building month built for uncovering the beauty in boundaries, January invites us to connect with our deck around themes of ownership, self-sovereignty, and competence.

    ZODIAC SIGN: Capricorn ♑

    ELEMENT: Earth

    QUALITY: Cardinal

    TAROT CARDS: the Devil, the World, the Ace/2/3/4 of Pentacles, and the Queen of Pentacles

FEBRUARY: THE MAGIC OF SPACE

An electrically charged closet cleanse for catalyzing change, February invites us to connect with our deck around themes of vision, space-making, and reinvention.

    ZODIAC SIGN: Aquarius ♒

    ELEMENT: Air

    QUALITY: Fixed

    TAROT CARDS: the Fool, the Star, the 5/6/7 of Swords, and the King of Swords

MARCH: THE MAGIC OF THE INVISIBLE

A touchy-feely pillow party for learning to love through loosening, March invites us to connect with our deck around themes of immersion, release, and evanescence.

    ZODIAC SIGN: Pisces ♓

    ELEMENT: Water

    QUALITY: Mutable

    TAROT CARDS: the Hanged One, the Moon, the 8/9/10 of Cups, and the Knight of Cups

APRIL: THE MAGIC OF VITALITY

An engine-revving starting line of courageous aliveness, April invites us to connect with our deck around themes of initiation, innocence, and impact.

    ZODIAC SIGN: Aries ♈

    ELEMENT: Fire

    QUALITY: Cardinal

    TAROT CARDS: the Emperor, the Tower, the Ace/2/3/4 of Wands, the Queen of Wands, and the Pages

MAY: THE MAGIC OF RIPENESS

A plush buffet of earthly delights fashioned from the tangible trust in our right to taste them, May invites us to connect with our deck around themes of worthiness, sensuality, and ease.

    ZODIAC SIGN: Taurus ♉

    ELEMENT: Earth

    QUALITY: Fixed

    TAROT CARDS: the Empress, the Hierophant, the 5/6/7 of Pentacles, and the King of Pentacles

JUNE: THE MAGIC OF BREATH

On butterfly wings fit for flying through every shade of the rainbow, June invites us to connect with our deck around themes of curiosity, exchange, and creative channeling.

    ZODIAC SIGN: Gemini ♊

    ELEMENT: Air

    QUALITY: Mutable

    TAROT CARDS: the Magician, the Lovers, the 8/9/10 of Swords, and the Knight of Swords

JULY: THE MAGIC OF SANCTUARY

A secret seashell of tender tending and deep listening, July invites us to connect with our deck around themes of protection, belonging, and emotional cycles.

ZODIAC SIGN: Cancer ♋
ELEMENT: Water
QUALITY: Cardinal
TAROT CARDS: the High Priestess, the Chariot, the Ace/2/3/4 of Cups, and the Queen of Cups

AUGUST: THE MAGIC OF ROMANCE

A bedazzled tropical trip for pulsing forward, pumping heart first, August invites us to connect with our deck around themes of passion, self-expression, and exposure.

ZODIAC SIGN: Leo ♌
ELEMENT: Fire
QUALITY: Fixed
TAROT CARDS: Strength, the Sun, the 5/6/7 of Wands, and the King of Wands

SEPTEMBER: THE MAGIC OF DEVOTION

A carefully considered chance to bow down to our nature and nature itself, September invites us to connect with our deck around themes of integrity, alchemy, and craft.

ZODIAC SIGN: Virgo ♍
ELEMENT: Earth
QUALITY: Mutable
TAROT CARDS: the Hermit, the Magician, the 8/9/10 of Pentacles, and the Knight of Pentacles

OCTOBER: THE MAGIC OF LIGHT

A serene sightline illuminating both what's here and what's possible, October invites us to connect with our deck around themes of reflection, alignment, and equilibrium.

ZODIAC SIGN: Libra ♎
ELEMENT: Air
QUALITY: Cardinal
TAROT CARDS: Justice, the Empress, the Ace/2/3/4 of Swords, and the Queen of Swords

NOVEMBER: THE MAGIC OF THE ETERNAL

A deep dive into the desire nature that makes us oh so human, November invites us to connect with our deck around themes of intimacy, power, and transformation.

ZODIAC SIGN: Scorpio ♏
ELEMENT: Water
QUALITY: Fixed
TAROT CARDS: Death, Judgment, the 5/6/7 of Cups, and the King of Cups

DECEMBER: THE MAGIC OF WILDNESS

A footloose confetti fest that frolics far beyond the unmapped roads, December invites us to connect with our deck around themes of celebration, faith, and risk.

ZODIAC SIGN: Sagittarius ♐
ELEMENT: Fire
QUALITY: Mutable
TAROT CARDS: the Wheel of Fortune, Temperance, the 8/9/10 of Wands, and the Knight of Wands

A Love Note from Your Deck

....

Like any love story, your journey through this tome will be utterly bespoke and will unfold most silkily when you step forward with your heart beating and your own intuitive instincts honed. Maybe you'll want to **proceed through the months** in chronological order and keep to the three-part card party calendar—first wandering the Majors' soul-sized climates to get acclimated; then heeding the Minors' calls to action; and finally, letting the Court graduate you into a way of being. Or maybe you'll want to scrap the straight lines and time travel instead, touching in with your birth month or zodiac sign's energies (note that if you're born near the end of the month, these might not be the same thing), or those of a beloved. Or you might find yourself in a "soul season" rather than a calendar season, connecting with a particular month's energetic themes and hanging with those card cuties for a while, regardless of the calendar date. Trust that your timing is always right on time.

You can play with both **intentional pulls** and **blind pulls**: plucking certain cards out and propping them up to commune with consciously, as well as seeing what pops up through facedown shuffles. In essence, the same psychic charge runs through both of these actions, we just access it through different layers of our being. Neither is a "truer" or "realer" reveal than the other.

This book doesn't explicitly illuminate different meanings for **card reversals** (when we pull a card that appears to be upside down), built on the belief that each card has a basic feeling tone and then infinite variations for us to intuitively explore. Track your own prism-facets as you pull. Maybe you'll notice certain through-threads for reversals. And maybe you'll also start to notice other, invisibly in-between angles. No matter the position of the picture, its energy might show up sideways in your hands—encouraging you beyond an either/or meaning of up versus down, and deeper into the all-around-the-town-ness of your felt experience.

While you're at it, don't worry about **choosing the perfect deck** or refining **your shuffle** to a fine art. Just pick a pack of cards that looks into your eyes and that you want to clasp hands with and hold close. While iconography is a rich and integral part of tarot's history and purpose, its seventy-eight archetypes also exist regardless of their visual presentation. In a pinch, you can even go deckless: writing the seventy-eight names on the back of index cards and pulling from the pile. Mix and mash them up however you like as you shuffle. And don't worry about readying or ritualizing your space or yourself for a pull, unless that feels powerfully celebratory to you. You can pull cards on a moving train, in the middle of a fight, and even when your hair is dirty. Tarot is no different from life. It *is* life itself. So go ahead and let it live.

Whatever your wild style, know that these seventy-eight friends are here for you and you alone. As you continue to work with them, you can start to see them as your biggest fans. Your sometimes tough—and always tender—champions, whose sole purpose is to help you shimmy through all kinds of weather. Clutch your deck to your chest. Sniff it like a bouquet of flowers. Confess your secret hopes and fears to it after midnight, and let it whisper back. It's yours to have and to hold for this one-and-only life. Like any intimate relationship, the more you commit to showing up to your deck in all your humanness— asking it to witness your hopes and fears; and receiving its feedback on a daily, weekly, and monthly basis, in keeping with the cosmos' bigger rhythms—the more wisely and deeply your deck will be able to love and support the ever-changing you.

Feel the weight of your deck. Hold the cards steady in your hands and acknowledge the time it's taken to get all the way to this very spot. As your year begins, January's cosmic energies want you to begin with the beauty of your bones . . .

This month's tarot cards cut our teeth on one question: *How will you handle your gravity?*

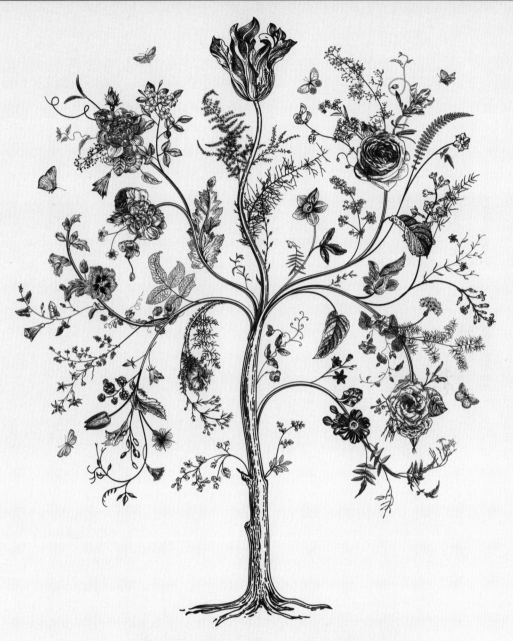

JANUARY

The Magic of Gravity

In the Stars: January is governed by the Cardinal Earth energy of Capricorn. Cardinal energy activates, and Earth energy fortifies. Gaining extra weight from its association with tough-love timekeeper planet Saturn, you can think about this month as a kind of ancient accumulation—stacking energy vertically like tree rings and giving life its finite architecture. A tangible way to access what Capricorn energy feels like is to explore gravity itself: sensing the downward pressure that courses from the crown of your head through the soles of your feet. Down from the heavens and through to the dust. That is you.

In the Cards: January's cardstock is made of calcium-rich stuff, and each of its seven archetypes asks you to stake a competent claim to your "still-here" status—inviting you to explore your sovereignty, self-sufficiency, and capacity to endure whatever the situation. These cards represent our soul survival: the continuation of life in the face of everything it's taken to get us here and to keep us standing vertical. They are the deck's bone-builders. Let them help you transform any perceived struggles into high-quality material that's made for the long haul: mining diamonds from your own luxe lineage of living.

In Your Life: To root you firmly in January's teachings, you can embrace a **daily practice** of "weighing in"—noticing what you're putting the weight of your time and effort behind; what matters most right now; how you hold your own history; and what kind of legacy you're leaving. Let January be a month for savoring the hard-earned products of your life—stepping out of the driving snow and safely into the ski lodge to sip on the 100 percent cacao elixir of your own experience. And let it also be a time for keeping your spine intact— restoring yourself to regalness so you'll be ready to face whatever the world has in store for you.

Whatever you've been through. Whatever it's taken. And whatever matter you're made from— it's yours for life.

ZODIAC SIGN: Capricorn
ELEMENT: Earth
QUALITY: Cardinal
CARDS: the Devil; the World;
Ace/2/3/4 of Pentacles; the
Queen of Pentacles
MAGIC WORDS: Bones.
Sovereignty. Competence.
Quality. Legacy.

MAJOR ARCANA

Take the first few weeks of the month to land in these card landscapes—orienting yourself to their themes and exploring their turf through meditation and visualization. You may also want to return to the inquiry questions as part of your daily practice.

The Devil + The World

January's duet of Major Arcana deities ushers us into the tarot's most self-sovereign of seasons. When we pull these cards, or choose to work with them intentionally, we are serving ourselves a crystal goblet of bone-building broth that beckons us to *remineralize our lives*. With their backing, we can give ourselves permission to receive the vitamin-rich residue of our time spent on earth: learning to love the lines that life has left on our palms, and refusing to let anything rob us of the precious gems of our existence in its entirety.

THE DEVIL: Unzipped Living

Stepping into this card's climate might make us feel hot and bothered at first. The Devil is that scratchy fabric that forces our bodies to sweat and squirm like we've come to the party dressed all wrong—overly starched and stiff in elaborate corsetry, or too exposed in our body-hugging frock for all to see. We might think we hear whispers from behind guests' cocktail napkins as we fumble with our canapés and spill the champagne. The Devil can make us feel like we don't quite belong—not even in our own skin—and can give us the impulse to escape rather than face the deeper sources of our discomfort.

When we begin to look around this archetype's landscape, the outside world may seem to be watching, assessing, and placing our passions on a good-bad binary. This can leave us feeling like external forces have the right to grant or remove our title as "decent human being worthy of love" in accordance with our performance of an impossible myriad of "shoulds." The Devil is this unending effort: we hope that if we keep at it, one day we'll be given a lifetime membership to some secret club of forever okayness. But we

XV

THE DEVIL

simply can't keep up with externally imposed standards. They're exhausting.

That's because the real energy of this card doesn't actually live anywhere outside of us. The Devil symbolizes an evolutionary empowerment opportunity, but that power doesn't lie in our capacity to fit ourselves into one-size-too-small clothes, or to win a bunch of nominal friends with a tight smile on our lips and hollow laughter in our heart. The Devil can't help us grow if we spend our lives falling into line by trying to internalize the laser gaze of those around us. Don't suck in. Don't hold back. Instead, unzip: strip off those shoulds, throw your stilettos against the brocaded walls like darts, climb onto the white linen tabletops, and maybe even leap for the chandelier. If you want to take advantage of Devil energy, get ready to spin naked for all the world to see.

Whenever we work with this card, the core of the Devil's treasures rests in our ability to assert that there are **no wrong desires**. There are no right or wrong moves. Silence the caustic commentary on your choices that might bubble up unbidden in your brain. And know that no one and nothing outside of you can call the shots. When the Devil comes through, it's here to cleanse us of any sense of shame so that we can stand with ourselves, no matter what state we find ourselves in. Yes, there will be moments in life where we're asked to course-correct. There are times when we should ask for forgiveness, bowing to the needs and expectations of others and letting other entities take the lead. But January is about spending some time in Devil country: striking the very notion of sinfulness from the score, and restoring yourself to the full sweet and sordid scent of your humanity. With this card, we mortar-and-pestle any anxious feelings of having to "make good" into a poultice that empowers our self-governed bodies.

 TURF TIP Explore the Devil through landscapes where the buttoned-up brushes against the more beast-like. Think after-work parties, afterhours clubs, wedding dance floors, and displays of emotion in public places.

ASK YOURSELF:

What are my "shoulds," and who is defining them?

Where does the seat of my power live? How do I exercise my own authority?

How do I relate to external pressures and the expectations of others?

Where am I ready to rebel—even, possibly, against my own outmoded expectations and standards for myself? What do I find shameful and where did I learn this?

If it was my last night on earth, what wild desires might I follow?

_____

_____

_____

_____

_____

_____

_____

_____

_____

_____

_____

_____

_____

_____

_____

_____

_____

THE WORLD: Legacy Work

Stepping into this card's climate can feel weighty and condensed, like everything that's happened in our life thus far is getting panini-pressed. It asks us to have and hold our entire earthly experience intact, receiving the full weight of its unfiltered energy. Hiking boots laced up as we peruse the turf we already possess, with our packs stocked with every memory—not one love letter left behind—we set out on our new year's journey. The World is a culmination, but also a reminder to ground ourselves in the wisdom of all that's gone down, because we're getting ready to get good with leaving it all behind.

The World is the heaviest hitter in the whole of the deck, an invitation to lift the heft of our histories and find the wholeness therein, no matter what we've done, or think we've left undone. It is also about owning up to the finite quality of our human lives: the end of our time on this planet. But you don't have to feel oppressed by your own mortality. Heaviness and gravity can be hard to bear, but they are also synonyms for vitality and value. In that sense, the World card's most powerful message is about our ability **to bear the weight of our own world**. The World pushes us to claim ownership over everything we've put our weight behind while also being aware of, and working within, our limitations.

Sometimes, drawing this card can signal the grand finale of a cycle of being we no longer have to be a part of. In these instances, the World helps us kiss some aspect of our tiny humanness a bittersweet goodbye. Other times, it might not mean that we are consciously closing the door on something, but are instead being beckoned into the colossal curtain call at the World's end: a celebration that reminds us that life's finiteness is what makes its finery so breathtaking. By using this card's energy, we can commit to picking up only the pieces that matter the very most when something falls apart. Whenever we deal with this final card in the Major Arcana, we find that when we face its limits, life can actually get lighter. Acknowledging all the hard-won hurts and carefully clutched happinesses, we open up to sticking to what matters to us for as long as we've got with all the strength we've got. That's all we can do, in the end: we've got to give up the rest to the glory of this gargantuan Gravitron to survive with our priorities intact.

Picture your sweet self in the slide reel of your life story, especially during moments of inevitable loss. See the photos of yourself in hotel rooms or empty apartments, about to shut the double doors for the final time and take your first steps into another as-of-yet-unknown beginning. Consider the duration of your life as an accumulation of these openings and shuttings. Our lives are the sounds of screen doors and car doors and plane doors: starts and finishes, beginnings and endings. Whenever we work with the World card, we're asked to inherit the whole of our warm-blooded existence. Yes, this is actually your life, says the World. So go ahead and climb on top.

 TURF TIP Explore the World through landscapes that are infused with historical grandeur and epic endurance. Think artist retrospectives, houses you used to inhabit, airport goodbye gates, and marathon finish lines.

ASK YOURSELF:

How do I face life's finiteness?

What courses have culminated in my current journey?

How do I work within the limits of time and my own abilities?

What matters most in this moment, and how can I more fully commit to putting my weight behind it?

If all of this is actually my life, exactly as it is, how can I celebrate it?

What would it look like to participate more fully in the whole of my existence?

What legacy is life leaving on me, and what legacies am I leaving behind?

_____

_____

_____

_____

_____

_____

_____

_____

_____

_____

_____

_____

_____

THE MINOR ARCANA

After exploring the big old biospheres of the Majors, you're ready to get nitty-gritty with the on-the-ground teachings of the Minors. Let the next few weeks of the month feel like a living laboratory as you practice responding to these cards by taking direct action, and noticing how they show up in your everyday life.

The Ace, 2, 3, and 4 of Pentacles:
DAILY PROVISIONS

As we learn to claim our own authority and legacy in the Devil and the World during January, we can look to this quartet of Minor Arcana card kiddies to figure out how to get good and grounded. Working actively with their energies helps us set ourselves up for life here on earth. Think of this foursome as *your trip to the hardware store*, where you'll gather the vital vittles that'll form your foundation for this month, and build the bedrock on which the rest of your year will bloom.

THE ACE OF PENTACLES

Each Ace in the tarot carries a gift basket of goodies in tow, asking us to receive and come alive to the element in question. Here, in the Earth element, we're asked to notice what's most useful in our lives, and to source tangible supports as a sign of good faith in our own continued competence. This card wants us to consider the miracle of itty-bitty breakfast-time acts that best build our bods for the long haul: eat your Wheaties so you can achieve your dreams.

What resources could I reach for right now that would fortify my body and spirit?

_____

_____

_____

_____

Tarot To-Do: Pen a super-simple list of five material-world things that you would add to a care package to yourself during hard times. These should be a few tangible items that would give you the strength to initiate when all you want to do is escape and collapse. You could add anything from pre-cooked meals made and ready for action in your freezer, to five minutes spent each morning striking a power pose in the mirror before you start your day.

THE 2 OF PENTACLES

Each 2 in the tarot wants us to slide between its Roman-numerical pillars and spark a journey of self-reliance that will take us through its entire suit. Here, in January's earthy, Capricorn-ruled 2, we're invited to own our expansions, and mature our majesty, by making like a plant or animal would as they drop brown leaves and slip out of constrictive cocoons with a Swan Lake–style spin. This 2 tells us that what no longer fits, or what we can no longer carry, is direct evidence that we're growing into our "adult" form.

Where am I naturally becoming bigger than something in my life, and how can I grow with greater ease?

_____

_____

_____

_____

Tarot To-Do: Imagine an area of life where you're outgrowing something and are hitting a natural limit in your ability to hold on. If there's a material symbol you can give to it—like a photo of a person or a page from a project—you might actually practice putting it physically down and pushing it aside. But rather than focusing on what you're getting rid of, place most of your energy on your current style of organic expansion. Stretch your limbs wide and bust out of your previous form, or imagine emerging from it as if you were stepping out of your clothes at the end of a hard day. As you embody your maturation process, you might even give a little shake like a wet pet coming in from the rain.

THE 3 OF PENTACLES

Each 3 in the tarot is a curvaceous bloom that exudes its already-good-enough essence. In January's 3, we are being asked to organically tailor ourselves toward life by relishing the roles that are really meant for us in each moment. Like kiddos unleashed onto a beach—immediately divining who's the bucket carrier and who's the hole digger—this card wants us to assume our position and perform it to the superhero hilt without feeling like we have to take on anyone else's tasks.

What is my role in life right now, and how can I relax into just doing "what I do"?

_____

_____

_____

Tarot To-Do: Imagine that you are giving yourself a title in your life right now, complete with an energetic job description. Maybe you're here to be "the excavator" in this moment, digging underneath and seeking to overturn old orders. Or maybe you're "the lover," here to infuse your world with soft-lit magenta heat. Whatever your title, practice moving through your day focused solely on the responsibilities of that role and leaving what's out of its purview aside.

THE 4 OF PENTACLES

Each 4 in the tarot offers us a hotel suite of protection, complete with the ability to take in only what we most want, ordering up room service at will. In January's ski lodge 4, we're asked to weatherproof our worth and settle securely into our center, losing no extraneous heat and letting nothing whip us into the winds outside. Our DIY den of do-not-disturb, the 4 of Pentacles asks us to increase our self-reliance and build a stalwart storm shelter from inner resources that are already on hand.

What actually feels good to guard against right now? How can I strengthen my walls and become more self-sufficient through self-containment?

_____

_____

_____

_____

_____

_____

_____

_____

_____

_____

Tarot To-Do: Imagine constructing your ideal weatherproof respite—fashioning the locks, ensuring the proper insulation and heating, and deciding exactly what kind of windows and curtains would help you feel best protected. While you're out in the world, you might practice erecting this structure in your mind whenever you feel put upon or pressured, drawing its shape around you and sketching yourself securely into your chosen quarters, whether it's a squishy iridescent bubble or a spiky star of safety.

THE COURT CARDS

Having acclimatized to the Majors' themes and lived out the Minors' on-the-ground energies, you're now ready to try the Court Cards on for size. Let the final few weeks of the month inspire an identity exploration: using the four "styles" sketched below to see how you're channeling this card's archetype, and/or adding your own way of embodying it to the list.

The Queen of Pentacles: GIVE YOURSELF GROUND

Each Queen in the tarot is a treasure-chest terrarium, beckoning us back into a secret space within us that's for our eyes only. In its earthy expression, this Queen is our escort into the heart of our majestic marrow. The Queen of Pentacles asks us to swap one-size-fits-all self-care solutions for the feel-good finery of tending our vessel in proprietary ways that actually feed our souls.

We can look for this Queen whenever we want to anchor to our root and flourish in the finite: activating this archetype to find the floor beneath our feet. No matter the life moment, we can start by reminding our toes that they have every right to relish a touch-down—sourcing sustainable, self-governed supports from the ground up.

Begin by stepping onto your piece of parquet, selecting from the floorboards below to help inspire your own stands for self-divined care.

Which style of grounding down best fits your form right now?

_____

_____

_____

_____

_____

_____

_____

_____

QUEEN OF PENTACLES

THE FOREST FLOOR. Maybe you want to touch down into the organics of life, taking your place in this elegant ecosystem and caring for self by leaning into supports that feel timeless and naturally selected. Imagine, or travel to, a plush emerald carpet where it's safe to slip off your shoes and bare your foot bones. Picture letting your toes tangle with the tendrils of trees.

THE SEA FLOOR. Maybe you want to touch down into the mysteries of life, taking your place in a flow of feelings and caring for self by tending the tidal shifts. Imagine, or travel to, the edge of the surf, the parquet of a swimming pool, or a see-through aquarium floor with fish beneath. Picture letting your toes stay solid amidst the ombré aqua morphs.

THE DANCE FLOOR. Maybe you want to touch down into the power of your own life, taking pride in your place as a showstopper and caring for self by expressing your singularity. Imagine, or travel to, a light-up floor that conjures rainbows with each step you take. Picture letting your toes relish their right to make an entrance.

THE PELVIC FLOOR. Maybe you want to touch down into the internal core of life, taking your place within the bowl of your own body and caring for self in a style that's completely self-contained. Imagine a seat springing up beneath your butt bones—whether it's a trapeze harness or a fully formed throne—and let your feet reach for the ground by first firming up this inner hold.

The Floor Plan Spread

....

This month is about setting yourself up well so you can handle whatever wildness arises in the year ahead. You've moved into your soul's home for the next twelve months: this super-simple spread is a great way to begin constructing the rooms where you will live. To bring this foundational energy to life, after you pull your four cards, you might fashion them into a little box for extra support, or even deposit them into each of their respective rooms in your actual house.

Note that although this spread talks about your "year ahead," tarot is actually your bestie for partnering with the present moment. Any calls into the future are really just invites to unfold toward a card's energy in the now and see what springs from there. If you notice yourself getting anxious about "what's to come" while you play with this spread, just swap references to "this year" for "this moment."

*Card 1: **The Kitchen.*** This card is here to help you feed your basic needs for this year—the fundamental flavor with which to stock your fridge.

*Card 2: **The Living Room.*** This card is here to help you fully inhabit your life this year—what you're being asked to "do" on the daily to ease into the comfy couch of your circumstances.

*Card 3: **The Bedroom.*** This card is here to help you build greater intimacy with your existence this year—a boudoir call to bare yourself to its archetype and come closer.

*Card 4: **The Bath.*** This card is here to help you cleanse and release this year—what wants to slide off your sudsy skin and gently down the drain.

* ✳ *

Building Your House of Cards

January's energies are all about fortifying our footholds and foundations. No matter whether you're a beginner or a well-seasoned card shark, you can take this time to go back to basics and build your mystical muscle. Start by dividing your deck into four piles according to element (in the Minor Arcana and Court Cards, the Pentacles are Earth, Swords are Air, Cups are Water, and Wands are Fire; for the Majors, you can use your monthly guide to divine their respective elements—the Devil and the World, for example, are Earth because they're both attributed to January's Earth-ruled Capricorn energy). Practice feeling into these elemental packs of cards and the energy they share, and observe the presence of these actual elements in the physical world around you (flip back to the Intro section for more on the elements). You might pull one card from each of the four elements and see how this quartet interacts and how you can invite each into your life—noticing which ones attract you more and which might feel spikier. You can also bone up on your basics by placing your cards in three packs—Majors, Minors, and Court Cards—and pulling a trinity from there. Let the Major represent the grander meaning of your situation; the Minor, the actions you might take to move through it; and the Court Card, the part of your identity that it's calling forth.

· ⇢ 👁 ⇠ ·

January Tarotscopes

CAPRICORN: *The World.* As the zodiac's most elegant survivor, you can summit in fur-lined style without breaking a sweat. January wants you to peruse all that exists on your palace grounds. Receive what's gone down before you push onward to expand your empire.

AQUARIUS: *The 4 of Pentacles.* You're an interstellar activist here to invite the world to exhale and expand past its edges. January wants to remind you that the inhale is just as vital. Protect your resources and take necessary restorative retreat so you don't deplete.

PISCES: *The 3 of Pentacles.* A boundless being here to dissolve the hard lines, you can empathetically teleport yourself anywhere. January wants to remind you that you're also a contoured force to be reckoned with. Identify and exalt in what only you can bring forward.

ARIES: *The Ace of Pentacles.* You're the zodiac's spark plug, here to kick off the whole shebang. But instead of having to remake the entire world from scratch every day, January wants you to stock your cabinet with self-renewing snacks. Set yourself up well with resources that run on autopilot.

TAURUS: *The 2 of Pentacles.* The diva of drinking it down to the last drop, you can take on any tasty that presents. January invites you to divine the difference between what you actually want to hold and the heavy weights you've been handling that are only keeping you down.

GEMINI: *The World.* You're a winged rainbow wonder, buzzing between sensation stations. January invites you to linger a little while longer. Remember that life is not just happening through you on its way elsewhere, but can also be delicious in its here-to-stay duration.

CANCER: *The 4 of Pentacles.* As the starscape's cozy cove, you're naturally inclined toward protecting vulnerable fishes. January's energies want you to care for your own competence as well. Build stronger seawalls that bring you closer to self-sufficiency.

LEO: *The 3 of Pentacles.* The zodiac's glitter kitten who leaves a trail of precious pawprints in your wake, you're here to feel your own heat. January wants to remind you that you can "do" you in even the most mundane of moments, shining on from wherever you stand.

VIRGO: *The Queen of Pentacles.* A coiled creatrix who metabolizes the world carefully, you're forever refining your approach. Take January to focus on your right to feel good without having to get results. Nourish your inner vineyards before you rush to bottle the juice.

LIBRA: *The Devil.* A luminous lifter who elevates life toward honeyed heights, you're here to mind the gap between actuality and aspiration. January reminds you that raw reality doesn't always have to be gussied up. Let embracing the grit lead you to even more glory.

SCORPIO: *The Ace of Pentacles.* You're a deep diver plunging toward intimacy, and January wants to remind you that closeness can come through cultivation. Practice building bonds with beloveds brick by brick without having to provoke others to feel them feeling you back.

SAGITTARIUS: *The Queen of Pentacles.* You're a wild desert pony here to stretch your limbs toward life's expanses. January wants you to power up for the outward adventures by stepping away from solid ground. Secure your self-care pack before you hit the open road.

As you depart January's ice palace and prepare to step into the width of February's sky, imagine placing your sweet self—and all the efforts you've made this month—in a clearing space, like a field or empty room. Notice how first staking a concrete claim to these qualities and accomplishments can help you start to open toward greater spaciousness.

Now, gather your January and February cards into two separate piles and pluck a pal from each pack. Lean into January's chosen card to hold you steady, and reach out toward February's friend to help you loosen your grip and learn to fly.

S pread your deck wider. Exhale past its edges into the empty expanse that clears the way for change. In February's width, your willingness to become panoramic provides a portal to another world . . .

This month's tarot cards electrify us with one inquiry: *What can you hold when you loosen your grip?*

FEBRUARY

The Magic of Space

In the Stars: February is electrified by the Fixed Air energy of Aquarius. Fixed energy widens, and Air energy expands awareness. Given extra room to move through its association with consciousness-clearing planet Uranus, you can think of this month as the swoop and then settle of a storm—finding freedom as what's outmoded gets emptied, and inhabiting the existential exhale and stillness of the aftermath before rushing to fill it. A tangible way to access what Aquarius energy feels like is to explore open vistas: standing with arms outstretched under a vast sky and taking your place as a participant in life's panorama.

In the Cards: February's cardstock is made of sweeping, spacious stuff, and each of its six archetypes asks you to clear the way for more life to come on through—forgoing sure things and hundred-proof absolutes, and letting it all "just happen" without getting too hung up on how exactly it's going to go down. These cards represent life's weather systems: here to broaden our perspectives and restore us to our rightful roles as part of a larger whole that can hold it all. They are the deck's visionaries and prophets. Let them untether you from what you think you know and whisk you forward into alternate futures.

In Your Life: To clear the way for February's teachings, you can embrace a **daily practice** of "meeting your edge"—noticing both what's known to you right now and what's unknown, without seeking to control either; and letting life show you what it wants to on its own time by allowing revelations to bob to the surface like perfectly cooked gnocchi. Let February be a month for renovation—whether it's a consciously conjured fairy-tale breeze that lifts you lightly out of your slippers; or a gale-force cyclone that sweeps you clean without so much as a weather warning. Whatever your winds of change, February is your time to make, take, and hold space for what arises.

You are all of this. And you are so much more.

ZODIAC SIGN: Aquarius
ELEMENT: Air
QUALITY: Fixed
CARDS: the Fool; the Star; the 5/6/7 of Swords; the King of Swords
MAGIC WORDS: Electricity. Renovation. Restoration. Witnessing. Biodiversity.

MAJOR ARCANA

Take the first few weeks of the month to land in these card landscapes—orienting yourself to their themes and exploring their turf through meditation and visualization. You may also want to return to the inquiry questions as part of your daily practice.

The Fool + The Star

February's duet of Major Arcana deities ushers us into the tarot's most expansive season. When we pull either of these cards, or choose to work with them intentionally, we set the tone for *cellular cleansing*. That means letting our stuck notions of how things are, how things could be, and even who we are, all get swept away by Spirit—a cellular cleansing restores us to an inner vastness that allows existence to simply unfold through our empty rooms with acceptance and even excitement. By welcoming in more and more kinds of weather without trying to protect ourselves against it, we become the whole of the sky.

THE FOOL: Making Friends with the Mystery

Stepping into this card's climate can feel like the drop of a roller coaster: the bottom falls out, and we're asked to forge some kind of funhouse faith in the fathomless-ness of life. It doesn't matter whether your hands are clenched tight on the bar or are outstretched into the cotton candy–scented air above. When you enter the Fool's domain, there is no GPS. No billboard signs, not even a trail of crumbs. Your dot drops off the map—you become utterly unfindable. The fundamental off-the-gridness of everything may leave you feeling hollowed out and shocked at first—obliterated by the realization that you're part of some existential nothing that's spinning nowhere at dizzying speed. You may grip the bar even more tightly, trying to feel your connection to something metallic and solid.

But any initial vertigo you'll feel when you investigate the Fool is only the start of a journey into a more boundless world. As you learn to let yourself bob up and down with the coaster's peaks and valleys, you will realize that you are actually beginning to embrace life's ebbs and

0

THE FOOL

flows. The Fool asks us: How will you make love to all this mystery? How will you bring your presence to this absence? Numerical card zero in our entire journey of seventy-eight, the Fool is here when we're asked to present ourselves to life for the very first time. Can we be down for it, no matter what *it* actually is?

Whenever we work with this card, we're invited to release rigidity somewhere in our lives and let our solid search for hard answers give way and create space for unexpected next moves. Maybe you want to know the truth about a relationship full of entrenched dynamics and endless dead ends. Or, you want to know what to do about a job where the mechanisms of your day in, day out leave you feeling robotic. The Fool arrives to push apart whatever's gotten stuck. And it achieves its work of "unsticking" by asking us to embrace both what's currently unknown to us, and what's ultimately unknowable—relinquishing our quest for easy answers in service of greater mystery.

Still, this card isn't here to blow up our lives or force us out of the plane into a skydive without a parachute. It won't ask you to leave your lovers and gamble away your 401K. Instead, it's simply here to remind us that **there is a trapdoor beneath everything**. However thoroughly we feel like we've figured out our situation, this card carries a current of "who the hell knows?" that can inspire about-faces and sudden course shifts. When we acknowledge that there is ground that wants to give way, we can let our perspectives widen into the open space instead of rushing to fill it like a problematic pothole. By being with the mystery, in the absence of the mappable, we make more room for magic—even if it's just for a fleeting moment. The Fool teaches us that when we lose the map, we find a new way.

 TURF TIP Explore the Fool through landscapes that are unmapped and unexpectedly aerated. Think altitude changes, off-the-grid zones, wind surfing, and the teetering space before the road rises to meet your next toe-tip.

ASK YOURSELF:

What is my relationship to mystery?

How do I respond when something is unknown or unknowable?

What is stuck in my life, and what is unsticking?

Where am I gripped, and where does whatever I'm grasping in my palm really long to go?

How does my own knowledge naturally arrive and recede without me forcing myself to figure it out?

Where is my growing edge of groundlessness right now?

_____

_____

_____

_____

_____

_____

_____

_____

_____

_____

_____

_____

_____

_____

THE STAR: Essential Restoration

When the world is almost asleep and the outline of each creature lies in stark relief against the violet sky, we enter into the climate of the Star. It is here, in this crepuscular light, that the Star begins to perform its therapeutic work upon us. Like an industrious nurse, it washes us clean and attends to our needs until the healing work gets done. It needles us with acupuncture until the energy flows freely. It massages the fascia of our feelings until we relax and reassemble. Often depicting a figure who's completely naked and engaged in a sacred act of ablution, this card wants to cleanse us back to the selves we were before all the accumulated beliefs and burdens of our lives left us gussied up in extra gunk.

When you check in to this soul spa, you might assume its restorative properties will always feel relaxing—a lavender-scented sauna, a silk robe, a sippy cup of prosecco. And there is absolutely nothing wrong with this fluff and plump approach to self-soothing. But remember that healing yourself can also mean excavating even deeper, unearthing yourself back to your original essence. Sometimes, this card can feel relentless in its efforts to strip us bare of all that has accumulated—more old-fashioned mountain sanatorium than upscale wellness retreat. But remember that however it presents itself to you, the energy of the Star always wants the best for you. Let this card be your reminder to take whatever you need from it to get back to who you truly are.

When our lives are difficult and we hold onto hurt, hard callouses can harden our hearts. The Star is sometimes about enduring fleeting discomfort to restore the tender skin of anger or sadness: these feelings want to be exposed so they can be tended to. Find your soft spots—they require attention. Buff yourself with pumice until your skin glows, even if it feels uncomfortable. If you feel oh so far away from some version of self you know is truer than the one you are embodying, the Star reminds you that you long to hold it close once again. On its quest to help us recover our original self, this card might also send us back to the source of a pattern in our life, so that we can get more clarity about how it all started.

Whenever we feel separated from a part of ourselves or a part of life, the Star wants to draw us back together again. It is a highly personal feeling that can manifest on many scales: whether we're seeking to soothe a hurt that's fractured our core self into pieces; or are simply craving an afternoon pick-me-up while picking up the literal or figurative pieces of a day that seems to have shattered. Whether we arrive to its energy feeling frayed and spent, or mostly intact, the Star is an invite to **plug back in to the sources that regenerate and renew us**—redressing and repairing whatever has become raw in service of the smoothness of our original self's softest, strongest skin.

TURF TIP Explore the Star through landscapes that are straightforwardly restorative. Think day spas, clear springs, brisk walks, and historic preservation sites.

ASK YOURSELF:

What has accumulated within me that wants to be exfoliated?

What are my sources of renewal, and how do I connect with them?

What wants to be traced back to its source?

Who is my original self, beneath all the residue of living, and what does this version of me need most?

What wants to be repaired and restored right now?

What holes want to be made whole; what hurts want to be healed?

_____

_____

_____

_____

_____

_____

_____

_____

_____

_____

_____

_____

_____

_____

THE MINOR ARCANA

After exploring the big old biospheres of the Majors, you're ready to get nitty-gritty with the on-the-ground teachings of the Minors. Let the next few weeks of the month feel like a living laboratory as you practice responding to these cards by taking direct action and noticing how they show up in your everyday life.

The 5, 6, and 7 of Swords:
CONSCIOUSNESS CHEMISTRY

As we learn to revel in the soul exfoliations of the Fool and the Star, we can look to this trio of Minor Arcana card kiddies to snip and clip stuck mental circuitry. Think of this trio as *your chemistry set*—a chance to experiment with the phenomena that set off reactions in your consciousness. You can use them to create vital space between life's triggers and your responses, and to forge clearer connections with what wants to be known right now.

THE 5 OF SWORDS

Each 5 in the tarot sends us cartwheeling through a room that seems small at first glance—banging up against the walls and learning to make the suit's energy our own through the rough-and-tumble mastery that comes from some healthy friction. Here, in the airy Swords suit, it's a chance to notice the light-up map of our reaction patterns. The 5 of Swords asks us to commune with the little pokes and provocations that life sends us. By first acknowledging them, we gain the space to decide how we'll choose to engage.

What situations, beliefs, and relationships seem to repeatedly set me off, and what purpose do my responses to them serve?

_____
_____
_____
_____
_____
_____
_____
_____
_____
_____
_____
_____
_____

Tarot To-Do: Imagine, or draw, one of those Rube Goldberg–style flow charts, starting with a few of your greatest "hits" at the top—people, places, and situations that send you sizzling in some way. Write out the chain reaction that occurs in the wake of each of these hits, noticing how your body, mind, and spirit respond, and bearing witness to this patterning without judgment.

THE 6 OF SWORDS

After the friction of the 5, each 6 in the tarot is a loving little ladle that wants to serve us life's renewable energy once again. In February's 6, we're invited to open up to the possibilities of circulation and allow any limited thinking to get reframed. The 6 of Swords throws back a sash on a stuck issue and slides open a screen door: bringing us alive to the fresh perspectives that arise when we let in the light and air of a 360-degree view and snack on our situation alfresco.

Which viewpoints might benefit from being given a new context or "take" right now?

_____

_____

_____

_____

_____

_____

_____

_____

_____

_____

_____

Tarot To-Do: Picture yourself carrying something that feels unbearably unsolvable to a park bench and dropping it off. If a stranger sat down beside the issue, what might they have to say about it? You might even play with literally translating your question or concern into a language you don't speak, simply receiving the reverberating sounds of recontextualization.

THE 7 OF SWORDS

The tarot's 7s coax us out of our comfy chairs and push us out the door of their element—they help us graduate into a new stage of being. In February's 7, we're asked to evolve our relationship with distraction. We can start by noticing the sparkly cat toy diversions that keep us questing after endless more-ness. By placing our attention on these attention-grabbers, this card helps us interrupt the busy spins and allow for more stillness to emerge. In this place of pause, what really wants our focus can come into clear relief.

How does the noise of my life sound right now, and what buzzes beneath it?

_____

_____

_____

_____

_____

_____

_____

_____

Tarot To-Do: Create an empowered parenthetical in your day. This could be a forced interruption in a mental spin. A temporary tech shutdown. A brisk walk around the block. Or just a lessening of some kind of excess more-ness—one less outfit accessory, one less binged streaming epi. As you summon the courage to create tiny interruptions in the white noise, notice what starts to sparkle up to the surface that's been longing for your loving attention.

THE COURT CARDS

Having acclimatized to the Majors' themes and lived out the Minors' on-the-ground energies, you're now ready to try the Court Cards on for size. Let the final few weeks of the month inspire an identity exploration: using the four "styles" sketched below to see how you're channeling this card's archetype, and/or adding your own way of embodying it to the list.

The King of Swords: WATCH THE WEATHER

Each King in the tarot is a space-maker and -taker—here to assume their fundamental right to exist by settling into their chosen seats with comfortable strength instead of anxious aggression. In its airy expression, this King imbues us with the power of panned-out presence, and escorts us into a place of neutral witness where we can start to let things happen *through* us instead of *to* us.

When we work with the King of Swords, we take responsibility for becoming panoramic instead of being possessed—allowing each life experience to be a chance to renovate a room of kneejerk responses, and to construct an edifice of consciousness that is big enough to let all the drama of our lives blow through without us getting blown to bits.

Tap this King by writing your own "weather report." You can start by observing your overall emotional state in this moment, or the particular conditions around a specific situation that's arising. Then, notice which of the four meteorological categories below feels most important to observe, and see if you can hold more space for whatever is unfolding.

Which parts of your life's current weather want more witnessing?

_____

_____

_____

_____

_____

KING OF SWORDS

TEMPERATURE. Notice what's pulsing hot and tropical, eager for your attention; and what's growing icier and more remote. Let yourself play with how to "insulate" toward different life happenings. Maybe the spicy bits want you to become barer, moving more intimately toward them. And the cold cubes could be asking for more bundling and self-protection.

PRECIPITATION. Sometimes we're super spongey with tears, getting power-washed by big fat splashy sheets of emotion. Other times, we exist in the arid stillness of more analytical distance. Notice how your emotions want to flow. Are you drenched in emotion right now, and does your mind need some drying out? Or are you parched with logic and in need of a little emotion?

WIND. All of our existence moves to the rhythm of storms, as our life's cloud cover comes together and catalyzes change, then becomes calm until we start the evolutionary shebang all over again. Notice what's building or settling within you right now; whether the winds are picking up for an all-out cloud clash, or if you're in a moment of stillness long after the uproar.

SUNLIGHT. Notice how much clarity is available to you. Maybe it's a clear turquoise sky of unified direction where you can see for miles. Or maybe you're in the midst of midnight, cloaked in a thick London fog and just waiting for the shape of something to arrive. Whatever state you're in, try neutralizing your relationship to what you can see and what you can't.

Mystery Meet Spread

This month asks us to embrace ever-shifting optics as we widen to hold both the known and the unknown. Allow this spread to be your square dance into the different quadrants of familiarity and unfamiliarity in your life right now. Take a singular issue, topic, or theme and let each card represent a different facet of it. You might select a life situation where you're feeling a little anxious and out of control in the face of some unknown aspect: like waiting for an answer about a job, or trying to figure out how another person might be feeling.

Play with seeing what it's like to adjust your zoom lens on the cards. You could start with the "known" cards close to you and the "unknown" cards farther away from you or even just out of view, and then move the cards in and out. What does it feel like to bring the "unknown" closer? What does it feel like to push the "known" farther away?

*Card 1: **The Sweet Known.*** This is the cozy, familiar groove in your situation's lounge chair. Assess which aspects of this card feel supportive and which might feel stifling.

*Card 2: **The Savory Known.*** This is the more piquant known in your situation—a persistent flavor that you absolutely know, but that some part of you really doesn't want to know or wishes you could ignore. Tread softly as you practice looking forward and away from this bit.

*Card 3: **The Sweet Unknown.*** This is your exhilarating edge—a bit of unknown that's really starting to rev up your soul's engine as you let its mystery embolden you. Pin it to your fridge and look forward to it like you would an exotic getaway.

*Card 4: **The Savory Unknown.*** This is an equally exhilarating edge, but one which you may feel more consciously fearful of approaching. Remind yourself that its spiced spikiness is here to awaken your senses and poke holes in old habit patterns rather than hurt you.

*Card 5: **Your Parachute.*** This is your aerodynamic assist in the situation—how you can learn to lean into its entirety and find a float.

Magic Trick:
Clearing Your Deck

February's energies are all about getting comfy with life's cleansings: seeing what new can come through when we let the old bits get whisked away. There are many sacred practices you might adopt to cleanse your deck—such as herbs, smoke, crystals, and sunlight. As you explore your approach, trust that no matter what you choose to do, your cards are always, ultimately, self-cleaning surfaces. There are no "bad" energies that are going to get permanently stuck inside of them or taint future pulls. There is only your own wisdom about how you might like to help energy move along through them. Sometimes, you might be traveling through a super heavy phase of life: reading for others or yourself in situations that feel weightily intense. Just like you might want a power-washing in the shower or a sweaty run outside after this kind of life experience, practice treating your deck just the same (maybe even placing it in a waterproof bag with you in the tub or strapping it to your back while your body bounds around the block). During other life moments, you'll just want to be left alone to self-regulate, and your deck will want the same. Know that you are made of the same stuff as it is, and carry it with you as you naturally clear the way.

February Tarotscopes

AQUARIUS: *The Star.* On your constant quest to electrify and overturn old orders, February is here to remind you that restoring something to its original form can be just as radical as tearing down to create anew. Let each act of renovation also be one of repair and return to what's essential.

PISCES: *The King of Swords.* You can sometimes feel crushed by your ability to take on the weight of others' worlds. But February wants you to explore how this capacity to hold space can power you up instead of making you feel invisible. Remember how vital your wide, open presence can be.

ARIES: *The 5 of Swords.* Your reaction time is almost instantaneous, as you spring to confront even the subtlest slights. February wants to help you neutralize these knee-jerk responses. Pause before you pounce, and check yourself before you wreak hot-blooded havoc.

TAURUS: *The Fool.* You're a hardy plant whose roots can flourish no matter the soil conditions. February invites you to trust so deeply in this internal solidity that you can loosen your foothold just a little. Find fertility in the flux and keep growing even amidst groundlessness.

GEMINI: *The 7 of Swords.* You are a star student who thrives on your ability to read the environment and respond accordingly, and February wants you to sharpen your focus. Spend time this month cutting through the static and honing in on the undeniable truths that insist on your undivided attention.

CANCER: *The 6 of Swords.* You can sometimes cling to life's photo albums, filled with tightly held stories of both pleasure and pain. February wants you to let the air in: update your old tales about the way it was, and let all participants, including yourself, grow and change over time.

LEO: *The 6 of Swords.* While you glean much of your magic by standing at the center of it all, February wants you to tap the power of the periphery. Instead of filtering each feeling through your personal perspective, become a creative champion who cheers the show on from every angle.

VIRGO: *The Fool.* You're the zodiac's alchemy apprentice: here to embrace the process of change. February wants to remind you that you don't have to scramble for solutions as things shift. Instead, let any unknowns strengthen your trust that you already possess the resources to respond.

LIBRA: *The 5 of Swords.* You can get caught in see-saw thinking, pressuring yourself into either/ors at every fork in the road. February wants you to break up the chemical patterns that keep you locked in this loop. Let new responses to old triggers present third and fourth ways to live.

SCORPIO: *The Star.* You've got an infamous capacity to unearth what's hidden, and February wants you to use it in the name of self-soothing. Identify the gritty bits of gunk you've been holding in your heart, draw them to the surface, and bubble-bath them on their way.

SAGITTARIUS: *The 7 of Swords.* A megawatt magic maker, you're forever chasing the tail of just a little more life. February is here to let you see that less-ness can paradoxically give you more. Cut away unnecessary attachments that only distract and clear the way for grand plans.

CAPRICORN: *The King of Swords.* The power of your presence is palatial, without you ever having to prove it. February is your call to enter every room as if you are the very walls that hold it up. Let this act of widening and bearing witness help fortify the unshakeable force that is you.

As you depart February's 360-degree sky lounge and prepare to step into March's invisible ethers, picture the "not-there" meeting up with the "here." Notice the unspoken currents, auras, and atmospheres that are intangible, but are undeniably present in your life's rooms. Imagine that they are as touchably real and alive as the wooden floorboards and ruffled curtains.

Now, gather your February and March cards into two separate piles and pluck a pal from each pack. Use February's card to clear your consciousness of any remaining constrictions, and let March's friend loosen you into loving even more.

L et every last card of your deck slip
through your hands. Watch whatever you're holding fast to flutter
away from your grasp as you flip them. In
March's fantasy fog, the undoing can be just
as vital as the doing . . .

This month's tarot cards whisk us away:
What have you got to lose?

MARCH

The Magic of the Invisible

In the Stars: March is infused with the Mutable Water energy of Pisces. Mutable energy loosens, and Water energy carries us away. The grand finale of the astrological year—which runs at a different rhythm from the calendar year, and is poised to start anew at month's end in Aries equinox energy—March is a melty moment imbued with the gauzy going, going, gone-ness of its ruling planet, Neptune. A tangible way to access what Pisces energy feels like is to explore life's constant fade-outs. Watch a friend depart from your arms after a candlelit dinner. Witness the sun melting into orange sherbet below the horizon. Observe a pad of butter dissolving into cream. You are learning to lose all the time. And that losing can become just another synonym for loosening—a language of love that lets the world come and go of its own accord for as long as it lasts.

In the Cards: March's cardstock is made from misty, moody stuff, and each of its six archetypes is an ombré opportunity to dissolve and undo life's hard edges. These cards represent the currents of the unseen world that exist all around us: the invisible, intuitive auras and atmospheres that often remain unspoken and are even untranslatable, but are powerfully present through feeling. They are the deck's psychic mediums. Let them help you become a séance of self: allowing all of life's inexplicably strange comings and goings to speak to you and through you without having to hold on to the "how" or even the "why."

In Your Life: To help you give in to March's fluidity, you can embrace a **daily practice** of "immersion in the invisible": tending endings and letting rigid resentments soften and start to slip away; allowing for the evanescence of people, places, and feelings; and following your "sense" of things wherever it leads—even, and especially, when you can't explain it. March is your moment to let it all fall apart just a little—no longer exhausting yourself by having to hang onto or hold up the sharpest sunlit version of things, and losing yourself in the boundaryless thrall. What is leaving you right now? What are you leaving? Could you let it all learn to swim?

ZODIAC SIGN: Pisces
ELEMENT: Water
QUALITY: Mutable
CARDS: the Hanged One; the Moon; the 8/9/10 of Cups; the Knight of Cups
MAGIC WORDS: Immersion. Evanescence. Undoing. Atmosphere. Endings.

MAJOR ARCANA

Take the first few weeks of the month to land in these card landscapes—orienting yourself to their themes and exploring their turf through meditation and visualization. You may also want to return to the inquiry questions as part of your daily practice.

The Hanged One + The Moon

March's duet of Major Arcana deities dips us in the tarot's slipperiest season. When we pull these cards, or choose to work with them intentionally, we *dissolve our resistance* to life's pushes and pulls and start to move in wilder ways: no longer forcing ourselves to get over the past or get on with the future. These cards are about getting good with getting under, alongside, and with whatever arises, instead. In this squishy, spirally space, there is no failure, falling behind, or forced fixing—only the wondrous process of becoming, which continues eternally, no matter what active efforts we make.

THE HANGED ONE: Suspended Animation

Slipping into the card's climate might feel motionless and muggy at first. You pick your arm up to grasp something you think you want and it falls back to your side, inanimate. Something seems to have ground to a halt, so you believe you've got to do something, anything, to get it going once again. You fear that if you don't force the forward momentum, you'll be left far behind as everyone else loves and lives and changes toward bigger, better versions of themselves while you shrivel and wilt. But what might happen if you just … did nothing?

This card's landscape is far beyond the reach of proactive power moves. Its energy is the paradox of **getting "done" by doing nothing**. And as it starts to undo our sense of efforting, we find that rather than punitive stasis, it offers an opportunity to let whatever our stuck situation change *us* while we wait for it to change. Hanging out in midair like a circus performer tethered by invisible string, we start to glimpse this life moment's meaning from unexpected

XII

THE HANGED ONE

angles: becoming available to mine hidden magic from it; separating the mirages from the meat of the matter; and only then, letting it fall away when we're actually complete with our current state.

However and whenever it comes through to us, the Hanged One always speaks to our beliefs about where we long to be in the linear timeline of our lives. We may pull it when we think we're done. Or it may arrive when we absolutely don't want to leave the land we're now living in—clinging with all our hearts to something we're holding onto. The Hanged One's energy slowly, invisibly wears away at our resistance. Wherever we find ourselves on the continuum between wanting to hold fast and wanting to let loose, this card asks us to open up and let life "do unto" us, too. It allows for the possibility that we may need to complete our stay in the hotel of our present state of affairs before we rush to check out. You may think you're done with a job, a relationship, or a lingering problem, but it might not be done with you yet.

When we let ourselves inhabit stasis, we discover the secret pulsations that are always moving through everything that surrounds us. We suddenly wake up to the invisible work that happens while we're fast asleep: all the little machinations of the world that we might not normally have noticed, performing their imperceptible magic like a nighttime beauty cream while we rest. Whether it arrives with regard to a relationship, professional endeavor, or way of being in the world, the Hanged One always signals that there's more to be done by letting ourselves become undone—letting life do its work on us without having to do anything at all.

 TURF TIP Explore the Hanged One through landscapes that are seemingly static but still invisibly alive. Think sensory deprivation tanks, waiting rooms, time-lapse photo frames, and chandeliers.

ASK YOURSELF:

What feels "stuck"?

What do I believe will happen if I remain in this place?

What timelines am I expecting, and which timelines are actually here?

Where can I perceive movement in the invisible realm: shifts in emotions, dream work, and the support of unseen, energetic allies?

If I were to write three lists—"to-do," "to-undo," and "to-not-do"—which areas of my life would ask for application of effort? Which would ask to be dissolved and released? Which would ask to be left alone?

_____

_____

_____

_____

_____

_____

_____

_____

_____

_____

_____

_____

_____

_____

_____

THE MOON: Midnight Snacks

When we enter the climate of the Moon, it is long after midnight. We're somewhere in the inky darkness and we find ourselves sleepwalking in zigzags through the wet seagrass of memory. The Moon is an echo from beyond. A pull from elsewhere. In this card, we are on our way to the kitchen in search of a snack we don't even remember wanting—navigating by touch, taste, and smell instead of conscious and rational thought. The swimming pool floor slopes off and suddenly we're in the deep end.

We might feel wobbly as we wade through the whirl-pool toward something we want but can't explain. But when we give ourselves over to this after-midnight edition of our self—no longer resisting the inexplicable and overwhelming, and getting just a little bit lost in our own deep-down deep end—we discover that wobbliness shows us our wildness. Just when we think we might go under, we instead find ourselves bobbing along in the sea of our own sensations, feeling big feelings, discovering options we never even knew we had.

Wherever this card shows up, it wants us to take a trip into the turf we might initially fear to tread. The megawatt emotional charges that pop out from behind trees to overtake us—plus-sized primal anger, tears, grief, joy—are often set off by life circumstances that may seem small by comparison. Howling echoes of memory from earlier in this lifetime and beyond call us down, down, down to the past life slideshow sensations we might want to be free of. All of the residue just beneath life's surface may feel like too much to deal with. But the Moon is absolutely not here to scare you straight or hurt you with its hauntings. Instead, it wants you **to become a practitioner of the paranormal within you**. It urges you to notice the moments where you feel possessed by the uncontrollable and to accept that they are part of you. Invite your ghosts in from the cold. Find out what tall tales they have to tell and ask them what they'd like to eat.

Whenever we work with the Moon card, we're asked to welcome in these woozy emotions and learn to bow to the forces from within and without that feel bigger than us, even if they disorient our sense of straight lines and step-by-step progress. The Moon invites us to let ourselves get carried out by these currents just a little, sensitizing ourselves to all of our tender, strange spots without feeling the instant need to fix them. If we temporarily lose sight of the shoreline, it's in favor of a different flavor of way-finding. We don't have to get better at navigating the dark, says the Moon. We don't need to gain more mastery over the so-called monsters. Instead, we just have to learn new ways to swim.

 TURF TIP Explore the Moon through landscapes that are uncannily insistent and beyond your rational grip. Think haunted houses, pitch-black places without light pollution, deep pools, and desert mirages.

How do I respond to emotions I can't explain?

What feelings overwhelm me and why?

What does it feel like to let myself get "taken" by strong emotions within me? How could I let myself be carried by these currents, and what would happen?

How do I usually find my way in disorienting situations, and what do I do when I can't?

What symbols and situations seem to keep returning back into my life, even though I might feel like I'm finished with them? What do these echoes want to tell me?

_____

_____

_____

_____

_____

_____

_____

_____

_____

_____

_____

_____

_____

_____

_____

_____

_____

THE MINOR ARCANA

After exploring the big old biospheres of the Majors, you're ready to get nitty-gritty with the on-the-ground teachings of the Minors. Let the next few weeks of the month feel like a living laboratory as you practice responding to these cards by taking direct action and noticing how they show up in your everyday life.

The 8, 9, and 10 of Cups:
DISAPPEARING ACTS

As we slip away into the endless oceans of undoing that are symbolized by the Hanged One and the Moon, we can look to this trio of Minor Arcana cards to help us consciously choose our own healthy escapes. You can think of these three as your *emotional elopements* and use each card to assess where you might want to engage in some good-for-you ghosting: disappearing away from your surroundings, off into a fantasy, or into full fusion with the present moment.

THE 8 OF CUPS

Each 8 in the tarot is a double-bubble infinity loop that asks us to remain in process and get softened by the elements. Here, in the watery Cups suit, the 8 is a perfect moment for learning how to simply fade away from a pattern or circumstance that we sense no longer quite serves our heart song. Without having to explain our reasoning or leave any info behind about where we're heading, the 8 of Cups is about slipping out the back door for a sojourn with self that answers the call of our inner siren.

What am I being called to fade away from; and how can I love it, and myself, through the leaving?

_____

_____

_____

_____

_____

_____

_____

_____

_____

Tarot To-Do: Imagine that you could turn down the saturation on a situation in your life, departing from it gradually, without conflict or confrontation. The situation in question doesn't need to be something that's explicitly "bad" or "wrong," but could instead be something that you just feel is no longer fully working for you. Picture the conditions of your departure. What time of day would you leave? What would you pack with you? What would you write in the love note you leave behind? What kind of vehicle would carry you out and away?

THE 9 OF CUPS

Each 9 in the tarot is a private treehouse where we climb for solitude. Here, in March's 9, our tree-house reaches up toward the stars, and we're asked to mix up a magic potion of hopes, dreams, and wishes for some wonder that's not yet here. It can sometimes feel wildly confronting to hope, as we immediately rush to protect ourselves from potentially not getting. The 9 of Cups asks us to linger in this space of wishing and let it open us: trusting that we are divinely deserving of our own dreams, and can bring the very best out of life by believing in them.

What am I most hoping for, even if I've never ever had it before?

_____
_____
_____
_____
_____
_____
_____
_____
_____
_____
_____

Tarot To-Do: Imagine yourself making a wish, then watching it come into focus as it arrives from afar. Even if the exercise feels silly at first, immerse yourself in the feeling of dreams beginning to come true. What fears do you have about feeling into your own fairy tales? How could believing that they will be granted shift the way you move through the world in this very moment?

THE 10 OF CUPS

Each 10 in the tarot is a buffet table where we're invited to feast on the fullness of our journey through the suit. These cards celebrate the culmination of all the loves and losses that have lived through us with each course. In March's 10, it's a feast for formlessness, as we're invited to let the specter of inevitable loss bring us more fully into the here and now. By facing the reality that every thing will eventually evanesce, we can show up courageously and immerse ourselves in this precious present moment for as long as it lasts.

How can I lovingly lose myself in what's presenting right now?

_____

_____

_____

_____

_____

_____

_____

_____

_____

_____

Tarot To-Do: Imagine or enact an experience where you let yourself be "with" whatever is happening in a sensually psychedelic way. Maybe it's petting a soft animal. Or taking the first bite of your favorite food. Can you immerse yourself within this experience and give yourself over so completely to the moment—even for a second— that you don't fear its finale?

THE COURT CARDS

Having acclimatized to the Majors' themes and lived out the Minors' on-the-ground energies, you're now ready to try the Court Cards on for size. Let the final few weeks of the month inspire an identity exploration: using the four "styles" sketched below to see how you're channeling this card's archetype, and/or adding your own way of embodying it to the list.

The Knight of Cups: FIND YOUR FLOW

Each Knight in the tarot is here to help us step in time to whatever rhythms pump out of life's speakers right now. The Knights bolster our ability to take what is happening in our lives in stride, finding our power by walking "their way." In its watery Cups expression, March's Knight reminds us that, whether or not we particularly like what's emotionally unfolding in life right now, we can relax into it a bit and ride along as we see where it carries us.

When we work with the Knight of Cups, we find that power comes not only from pushing against, but also by "going with." Tap this Knight by considering how the waters of your life are asking you to move through them and selecting the maillot below that would best fit your swim.

How can you let go into the current flow?

_____

_____

_____

_____

_____

_____

_____

_____

_____

_____

KNIGHT OF CUPS

THE ONE-PIECE. Maybe life's shifting waters are asking for a classic, tried-and-true approach right now. Practice summoning familiar skills and resources you already have on hand, moving steadily through the situation by anchoring yourself in an image of internal wholeness.

THE STRING BIKINI. Maybe the wild waters are asking for more of your own energy. Practice participating in your life with your full body, letting the situation touch your bare skin without recoiling, and even finding some spring-break-beach-blanket fun in the flux-like flow of it all.

THE CAFTAN. Maybe beach time is more about hide-and-seek at this moment. Practice touching in with the situation's emotional currents for a little while, and then covering up and tucking under your umbrella when you need a respite.

THE SCUBA SUIT. Maybe life's waters are asking you to look a little deeper and you're ready to plumb the depths. Practice thickening your skin by creating a bit of distance—summoning protectants to ensure that you can pass through your situation without getting fully soaked.

Going, Going, Gone Spread

....

This month wants us to get good with life's goodbyes, and welcome the wiggly wonders that want to come into and out of our worlds, all on their own. Let this spread be your Slip 'N Slide, and pose a question about something that's leaving you—like a partnership that's reaching its natural denouement, or a habit pattern that's headed for the door. If nothing specific springs to mind, you can inquire more broadly about how to let things happen with greater ease.

You could even make this practice physical by writing the names of these cards on scraps of paper after you've pulled them. Practice "dissolving" the first three by dipping them in water and then letting their ink smear, shredding them, or leaving them outside to weather in the elements; and hang onto the fourth card's energy by placing its paper in a secure spot.

*Card 1: **Heading for the Door.*** This is the bit that's here to help you start your slip away from the stuckness of the present moment. It could represent what's starting to loosen and leave your situation, or it could be your escort—here to give you a little extra wiggle room to release. Let this card inspire you to begin accepting the inevitability of departure.

*Card 2: **Halfway Out the Door.*** This card represents the "hold" you might have on your situation—the sticky bit where you've started to seize up and grip tightly in the face of loosening. Just notice how you hang onto the message of this card. Try to get curious about why you think you've got to drag it back into the house instead of letting it leave and do its thing.

*Card 3: **Gone.*** This is the part of your situation that's fully receding from view. It could represent a quality that you no longer need to rely on, or a phase that's faded out. Notice how you feel as you face this card's absence; and see if you can trust that it's not necessary to lean on in this moment, and find relief in releasing it completely.

*Card 4: **What Remains.*** This is the eternal in your world right now—the love buddy who's safe and secure at home awaiting you with a plate of cookies, no matter what. You don't even need to hang onto it because it's already got you covered. Even if this feels like a card you would rather see gone, explore how its message might provide unexpected stability.

MAGIC TRICK:
Trusting Your Intuition

March's energies are all about releasing rigid rationalism and communicating with the invisible world. We're all imbued with intuitive capabilities that want to be nurtured, and we all have our own style of sensing what a card means for us. Maybe you're a physically sensitive soul who reads energy through the tactile world. In this case, you might practice fully immersing yourself in a card: softly gazing at it until the edges get blurry and you're "in it," or even dressing in its colors for the day. Or maybe you trend more ethereal, and want to lay a card beside your pillow at night and let it slip into your dreamscape, jotting down any visions the next morning to help you understand its meaning. Or, you could be an "aha moment" kind of creature who conjures magic out of thin air. In this case, you might practice "blind pulls" without your physical deck even on hand—just picturing the archetypes floating through space and seeing which card name naturally steps forward. Intuitive knowings about our deck can come through any and every sense. You could get a tingling in your body, hear a pop song playing, sniff bacon on the breeze, or see the color cobalt when you pull cards. Just practice staying open with all your senses and seeing what card meanings come calling, however they arrive.

March Tarotscopes

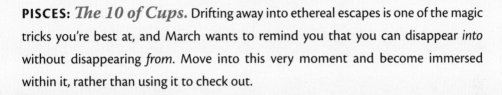

PISCES: *The 10 of Cups.* Drifting away into ethereal escapes is one of the magic tricks you're best at, and March wants to remind you that you can disappear *into* without disappearing *from*. Move into this very moment and become immersed within it, rather than using it to check out.

ARIES: *The Hanged One.* You're a verb of a human whose sense of self sometimes feels synonymous with your ability to "make it happen." March's cosmic landscape is here to open you to the many energies that want to move you, without you having to move a muscle.

TAURUS: *The 8 of Cups.* Your spirit loves sitting firmly at life's endless buffets. March wants to remind you that leaving the table for a little while can actually help you discern your next course. Instead of stuffing down whatever gets served up, take time off to work up an appetite.

GEMINI: *The 10 of Cups.* Sampling every shade of the rainbow is one of your superpowers. March wants you to embrace this status as an omnivore of experience. Trust that whatever you're fully feeling in this moment is worth immersing yourself in for however long it lasts.

CANCER: *The Moon.* You're an after-midnight mystic who can wade into the deep end wearing your boldest bikini, and March is here to help you get even more bottomless. Wild out in the flux of your own feelings without having to apologize to anyone for your tender tones.

LEO: *The 9 of Cups.* You love to clutch and caress life, holding it close to your chest with all your might. March's energies want to awaken you to what's far away as

well. Let your fantasies refresh your faith in the future, and hold out hope that there's even more magic to come.

VIRGO: *The Moon.* You find preciousness in each piece of life's puzzle, and March wants to complement this process by asking you to perceive the micro magic you can't see. Accept assists from the invisible world, and know that what you can't explain is also working on your behalf.

LIBRA: *The 8 of Cups.* You're forever limbo-ing under the effects of your causes. March wants to soothe your worries about the potential consequences of your actions. Honor your own wiggles away from whatever doesn't move you without having to anxiously anticipate the aftermath.

SCORPIO: *The 9 of Cups.* A seasoned traveler into life's spiky terrain, you're well-acquainted with sweetness that's hard-won. March wants to remind you that you also have the right to dessert before dinner, having at the honeyed good stuff without first proving you deserve it.

SAGITTARIUS: *The Knight of Cups.* You're a magic mover and shaker who comes alive when the solid ground gives way to the next adventure. March is here to help you find a flow that moves *with* what's unfolding, not just *toward* the next target.

AQUARIUS: *The Hanged One.* You're a star-gazing strategist who sees all of life's synchronicities from high above. March wants to open your third-eye even further by asking you to pause and look around. Keep your gaze soft and watch things reveal new sides as the hard edges dissolve.

CAPRICORN: *The Knight of Cups.* You get so much of your diamond grit by gritting your teeth and getting on with it. But March wants to remind you that you also have every right to get carried along for a little while. Allow the easeful moments to be just as fortifying as the frictional ones.

As you depart March's underwater ombré and head for April, notice how things come to life. The first streaks of sunrise. A dog unleashed with a case of the zoomies. Your own smile breaking through like a baby bud. All the nibbles of newness are nudging you, however microgreen their mojo.

Gather your March and April cards into two separate piles and pluck a pal from each pack. Allow March's card to soften you toward an inevitable ending and April's fresh pick to invigorate an unstoppable new start.

Check your deck's pulse and prime your card-pulling pump, because *this is it*. Flash each card like a start flag green-lighting the fact of your existence. In April's land of ignition, your pulse is your promise to keep it lit for as long as you live . . .

This month's tarot cards blaze into being with one insistent urge: *Just. Say. Yes.*

APRIL

The Magic of Vitality

In the Stars: April is injected with the Cardinal Fire energy of Aries. Cardinal energy champions, and Fire energy brings us more alive. Charged with the engine revs of ruling planet Mars, this is the itty-bitty baby bud of the astrological year, and the closest we'll ever get to life itself. No coulda-woulda-shoulda wobbles. No ifs, ands, or buts about it. Just bold beingness barreling out into the world with innocent ardor. A tangible way to access Aries energy is to explore animus: the neon chartreuse of tree leaves; the snappy click of heels leaving the house. There is life-force coursing through each and every thing that's alive, and you are here to be a part of it.

In the Cards: April's cardstock is made of sizzling, cinnamon stuff, and each of its seven archetypes (plus the Pages) is an invitation to collide, rub, and spark—letting yourself catch fire as you mingle with the unstoppable force that kindles all of life. These cards represent the persistence of existing: pulsing, pushing, and powering up and out through the pavement cracks. They are the deck's on switches and birth certificates. Move them and let them move you—worrying less about who or what seems to be "doing" the doing, and just throwing yourself into the pan to get good and done.

In Your Life: To unleash April's vitality, you can embrace a **daily practice** of noticing "verbness" in your life: the willpower that's present in the beings who surround you, and the delicious dents they deposit. Maybe it's your kiddo pushing a toy truck off the edge of the table. Or a colleague pushing an edit through on a vital document. Or your own body pushing through a thick crowd. April is your month to honor both impulse and its impact. And, rather than getting caught up in the complexities, to just let things rip: reveling in life's primary sensations, facing any fallout from inevitable clashes, and calling it like it is. A lean, clean, mojo machine, April's energy asks us to cut the fat, save the meat, and get the hell on with it.

ZODIAC SIGN: Aries
ELEMENT: Fire
QUALITY: Cardinal
CARDS: the Emperor; the Tower; the Ace/2/3/4 of Wands; the Queen of Wands; the Pages
MAGIC WORDS: Innocence. Friction. Libido. Immediacy. Force.

MAJOR ARCANA

Take the first few weeks of the month to land in these card landscapes—orienting yourself to their themes and exploring their turf through meditation and visualization. You may also want to return to the inquiry questions as part of your daily practice.

The Emperor + The Tower

April's duet of Major Arcana deities lays bare life's libido. These cards awaken us to *the forces that course through every being,* letting all of existence simply pump its blood without becoming a battleground. When we pull these cards, or choose to work with them intentionally, we take responsibility for our personal power, and appreciate the capabilities of the forces outside of us, too. The Emperor and the Tower ask us to respect all of the engines of creation that exist—accepting both our own bold birthright and life's larger impacts without having to play offense or defense.

THE EMPEROR: The Force of Us

We step into this card's climate and the grass blades bend in our wake. We drop into the Emperor's cushy chair, denting its plushness with our weight and daringly displacing even the most petite particles of air that surround us. We have arrived in this place, and there is no arguing with the fact of our existence. Just by existing, we have changed this world, and we're going to keep on changing it simply by our physical presence on its surface. We are here. There are no accidental entries to planet Earth.

When we find ourselves in a new situation, our reaction is often to try to find our place within it: responding by either backing down or forcing forward. We might blink back our bigness in this card—becoming shy and specklike. Or we may fly to the opposite, supersized end of the spectrum: inflating our effect so everything knows we're still vital to this mission—flexing and denting to ensure that our force hasn't been forgotten. Wherever we fall on this big-small spectrum, this card's energy wants us to stop apologizing for and scrambling to gather evidence

IV

THE EMPEROR

of our existence, and to start becoming "right sized" instead. That means inhabiting our fundamental footprint within our own life by taking up space that's naturally needed in each situation—neither diminishing ourselves nor dominating.

Whenever we work with this card, we're asked to consider the shape and size of our own force: the effect we always have on any given situation, however subtle that imprint might seem. Whether we've been supersizing it or shrinky-dinking it, the Emperor wants to remind us that **we bear both the right and responsibility to exist within our lives**. When you pull this card, maybe it refers to a partnership where you've foisted all of your feeling onto your beloved and have become empty of your own emotions. Or it could be about a job where you've been running the whole show without considering how the efforts of your colleagues have contributed. However it shows up, you're asked to look at how power is being apportioned in a situation, and to become more conscious of your own use of it.

Meditate on the Emperor by internalizing the concept that you are neither minuscule nor monolithic, but are exactly as you are. In this perfectly sized place, you don't have to play the dictator or the subject. Instead, show up in the skin you're in and take your place in this world without cowering or conquering. Stand upright on your self-granted ground and strike a power pose—you earned the right just by being born.

 TURF TIP Explore the Emperor through landscapes that are perfectly sized in their power. Think old-growth forest footprints, scaled dollhouse miniatures, community garden plots, and your seat at the table.

ASK YOURSELF:

What effect does my existence have on the world that surrounds me right now, and how could I get more comfortable with this effect?

When and why do I dull or mute the magnificence of my presence?

When and why do I amp up my existence in an effort to prove my power?

What would it mean to become "right sized" in my life, neither flexing my force nor shirking responsibility for my footprint?

_____

_____

_____

_____

_____

_____

_____

_____

_____

_____

_____

_____

_____

_____

_____

_____

_____

THE TOWER: The Force of Everything That Is Not Us

Arriving in this card's climate might feel like a shock to the system at first. With a roar, a crash, a strike, and a thundering of falling stonework, our forgone conclusions crumble. The Tower has a reputation for destruction that's perhaps unparalleled in the whole of the tarot deck—amplified by imagery that's often of a building getting blown to bits as bodies are sent flying. The Tower can loom large and come in hot. Even if we're well-seasoned practitioners who know intellectually that no card can spell doomsday or do anything "to us," we may still find our heart beating faster when this fiery friend comes calling.

But at its heart—and it does have one—the Tower is here to ravish us with the remembrance of the raw force inherent in everything. Sometimes we make moves in life. And sometimes we get moved. And there can be glorious meaning to be made in both styles of movement: whether we've consciously chosen a path and immediately grasp its import; or are able to understand the grander plan that a life event is part of, even if we didn't deliberately select it. But at other times, there is no meaning. Just life begetting life. The Tower reminds us that some things happen for a reason, and other things just happen.

This card is a companion for all of the flavors of force that exist. We may make sense of the things that happen to us, cataloging them into our epic life story with a clear understanding of what they mean. But then there are those out-of-nowhere, falling-from-the-sky rocks we can't ever explain, which leave their dents in broken bones and hardened hearts. The Tower **asks only that we become conscious of life's charges**. Sometimes this feels utterly exhilarating as we give up the controls. And at other times, we can't help but struggle for the scraps of whatever our worldview once was, grabbing at the shreds of our old life as it flies out the windows in the explosion. There's no "right way" to respond to this card's energy. The Tower has its own force, but it accepts ours as well. We can stand and fight. We can submit and slide under. We can wild out and make sweet love. The choice is ours!

Whenever we work with this card, it simply wants to bring us alive to all of the forces that surround us. The Tower is no inevitable cataclysm. No harbinger of full-scale destruction or reason to fear. Its energy can operate on any scale: it is the infinite variety of power plays present in any moment—here to remind us that life is not just a logical progression that we can always retain control of through absolute understanding, but a physical embodiment that we sometimes just need to *live*. We don't have to strategize our next move, or even make sense of what's gone down, for life to keep on moving and grooving through us. Swept clean of our attachment to who plays the hero, the Tower asks us to let ourselves get va-va-voomed by the muscle of the moment, feeling it in every vein.

 TURF TIP Explore the Tower through landscapes that unleash inevitable force. Think the starting blocks at a race, fireworks displays, geysers, and demolition derbies.

ASK YOURSELF:

What are all of the forces that are at play in my life right now? Which of these am I willingly participating in, and which am I resisting?

How do I respond to moments of conflict?

How do I decide when to push forward "against," and when to move "with"?

Which situations and happenings in my life want to be made sense of, and which want to be left alone—simply regarded and felt rather than analyzed?

_____

_____

_____

_____

_____

_____

_____

_____

_____

_____

_____

_____

_____

_____

_____

_____

_____

THE MINOR ARCANA

After exploring the big old biospheres of the Majors, you're ready to get nitty-gritty with the on-the-ground teachings of the Minors. Let the next few weeks of the month feel like a living laboratory as you practice responding to these cards by taking direct action and noticing how they show up in your everyday life.

The Ace, 2, 3, and 4 of Wands:
READY, SET, GO!

As we supercharge with the Emperor and the Tower's life-affirming forces, we can look to this quartet of Minor Arcana card kiddies to infuse our power moves with some eggshell-breaking innocence. Think of these cards as *your camping kit* for coming to life. Use each card to show you a different way to make sparks fly, as you brush up against life on the playground of empowerment and enjoy your own role in the process of creation.

THE ACE OF WANDS

Perhaps the most pared-down of the Aces, this primary-colored card is a straightforward on/off switch for all of existence. In its energy, we're asked to make life leaner by cutting the drama and cleaving the hot from the cold. When we notice what's most alive for us in the moment, we can give more of our precious life-force to it. This card wants us to become available to turn toward newness by turning on and tending the tiniest particles of passion we can find.

What spark wants to become a full-blown fire right now, and which embers are going out?

_____

_____

_____

_____

Tarot To-Do: Imagine that everything in your life has an on/off switch. When you examine certain emotions, projects, places, and people, which are currently turned "on" and which are "off" for you? Practice looking at each part of your life pragmatically, turning yourself toward what's on and away from what's off. You might even literally mark symbols of them with green and red Post-it notes to remind yourself of the green light and red light zones.

THE 2 OF WANDS

Each 2 is our chance to divine our direction through its element. In the Wands suit, symbolic of the Fire element, we've got two sticks and it's time to rub them. When we pull the 2 of Wands, we're giving ourselves a chance to experience the simple, exhilarating sensation of our singularity. This card wants to return us to that little-kid sensation of pushing off the pool wall or leaving our footprint in wet concrete—reminding us that just doing something, anything, can make us feel alive.

What one move could I make right now, however micro, to assert my role as the protagonist in my own life?

_____

_____

_____

_____

Tarot To-Do: Imagine something that's unfolding in your life right now where you feel you have no power to make an effect. Picture touching it with some part of your body. Maybe it's pressing a thumb into it. Or speaking one word of *no* or *yes* in the face of it. However seemingly small the act, imagine your effect dinging the surface of the situation and depositing a dent.

THE 3 OF WANDS

The luscious bubbles of the 3 in the element of Fire bring our hot pot to a rolling boil, and in this card, we're asked to raise the heat and the stakes. The 3 of Wands wants us to up the ante on our spirit's relentlessness, and let ourselves become fresh littles who are here to live and learn, again and again. This card is an opportunity to come at our next experience like neophytes without having to conquer or master it in a moment, taking our shot sans self-critique about our technique.

How could I become fresher in the face of challenge—letting myself just give it a go without fearing a screw-up?

_____

_____

_____

_____

Tarot To-Do: Imagine performing one thing you're a master of, and one thing you know nothing about, side by side on a dual screen. Notice the energy and attitude you apply to each. Then, picture the two screens compressing into one, as any anxiety about the area of inexperience blends seamlessly with the natural exuberance that comes with performing a mastered skill. What would it look like if you were able to apply the same approach to both activities, without any shred of self-assessment?

THE 4 OF WANDS

The 4s are an opportunity to check in to the hotel suite of self-reflection. Here in Fire, we're given the chance to actually experience and enjoy the effects of the energies we've put out into the world. We're often so caught up in enacting the next action that we forget to feel the worthy warmth of the efforts we've already made. This card invites us to receive the treats cooked by our own heat: acknowledging all of our attempts, noticing where we've done enough, and coasting on the momentum of our mojo.

Where have I done enough, and which of my efforts want honoring right now?

_____
_____
_____
_____
_____
_____
_____
_____
_____

Tarot To-Do: Imagine throwing a party to celebrate your efforts exactly as they are in this moment. Which would you choose to honor and how would you acknowledge them? Your mind might immediately go to the explicit "wins" you think are most worthy, but take some time to feel into the subtler parties of your personhood. What aspects of your ever-evolving endeavors want to be marked and enjoyed as more-than-enough right now?

THE COURT CARDS

Having acclimatized to the Majors' themes, and lived out the Minors' on-the-ground energies, you're now ready to try the Court Cards on for size. Let the final few weeks of the month inspire an identity exploration: using the four "styles" sketched below to see how you're channeling this card's archetype, and/or adding your own way of embodying it to the list.

The Queen of Wands: COME ALIVE

Each Queen in the tarot is a boudoir: an inner sanctum that brings us face-to-face with personalized feelings that nothing outside of us can replace and no one else can possess. In the Wands, this self-governed siren presides over our internal fire pit—guarding our style of self-expressive heat.

We can look for this Queen in our private experiences of fundamental aliveness. Those magic moments when we don't have to secure any tangible evidence of our efforts in the external world to know that we are still passionately present and accounted for: undeniably "here" and awake through every cell in our bodies. It speaks to the concept of "libido" writ large—not just as erotic drive, but as our right to relish the fiery fact of our own existence.

Tap this Queen by considering your own style of "coming to life"—using the sources below to inspire your inner ignitions, even when you might feel extinguished.

What kind of life-force lives in you?

_____

_____

_____

_____

_____

_____

_____

_____

QUEEN OF WANDS

THE SPARKLER. Maybe you're a person who comes to life suddenly, seemingly out of nowhere: party-ready for a special occasion, crackling out into the night sky. Explore what provokes your passion and "sets you off," and play with learning to enjoy both the appearance and evanescence of your flame, however it comes and goes.

THE OLYMPIC TORCH. Maybe you're a person who comes to life in the wide open, with lots of room to burn and no encumbrances to inhibit your eternal flame. Explore the freedom inherent in your fire, and play with how it survives and thrives in the face of opposition, running loose beyond the limits and rising to meet challenges.

THE SOLARIUM. Maybe you're a person who comes to life through cooler experiences of self-reflection and analysis, getting warmer as your consciousness and clarity increase. Explore how your powers of perception help you stoke your flames, and play with focusing your fire through "aha" moments and visions of new life appearing on the horizon.

THE BBQ PIT. Maybe you're a person who comes to life while being surrounded by warmth—celebrating the creature comforts of a contained hearth of heat. Explore the enveloping properties of your flame by noticing how you hold and retain passion, and play with drawing things closer to you and nourishing them through your loving touch.

Yes/No Spread

....

While life is certainly well-lived in the many rainbow shades, and it's wise to acknowledge the nuances that may escape us, April's energies give us an opportunity to be courageously concrete. Sometimes the right decision is just to go ahead and call the shots. Let this spread be your green light/red light when you're exhausted from equivocating and hesitating and just want your deck to give you something straight and strong.

Start by flipping half your deck (thirty-nine cards) faceup, keeping the other half downward facing. Then close your eyes, swirl the cards around, and feel into your yes/no question. Drag a card forward, open your eyes, and see if it's upward facing (a "yes") or downward facing (a "no").

You can dance into the deeper meaning of the card in a moment, but at first feel into the fundamental yes or no answer you've received. Rather than take this answer as a fait accompli that comes from outside of you, let it be like a coin flip, where if you get a "no" on something and find your heart sinking, you'll know that it might actually be a "yes" for you. Let this exercise remind you that you can use this feeling of friction to further clarify your own stance, and that your deck is never going to act upon you without your permission. After figuring out your answer, you can let the nuance of the card meaning help advise you on how to handle your decision.

Freshening Up with the Pages

Our bonus babies of the tarot, Pages don't roll up squarely under any particular cosmic season. In April, we can harness their energy at the starting line of the astrological year to invigorate ourselves with innocence. You can think of each of the Pages like a chance to freshen up after a long voyage by splashing some water on your weary face, or taking a brisk breath of air around the block. As you peruse the pack of four, you might want to turn them over and pluck one to see where you can open to the *newness of nowness*.

THE PAGE OF WANDS

This Page offers us the chance to look at our identities anew at any moment. Does that shade of lip gloss still symbolize our essence? Are we keen to keep that haircut or nickname? Use it to step into the powder room of personality and assess where you might be ready to see yourself through different eyes and rise to a new occasion. *Who are you right now?*

THE PAGE OF CUPS

This Page offers us the chance to look at our hearts anew at any moment. Yes, we've put them through it, scarring their tender surfaces. But the fluidity of fantasy can keep on changing the course of our emotional lives, no matter our age. Use it to experience your emotions with the imaginative innocence of a first crush—maybe even having some splashy fun with your feels. *What does your heart beat for right now?*

THE PAGE OF SWORDS

This Page offers us the chance to look at our consciousness anew at any moment. We may think we've got it all figured out, but this card's energy wants to crack us open to the surprise parties of perception. Use it to learn something new about your life and see what inspirations want to embolden you. *What can you see and say right now that you couldn't before?*

THE PAGE OF PENTACLES

This Page offers us the chance to meet the material world anew at any moment. It's a reminder that we've got the right to find delight in the simplest of sensations, and to be awed by our sensory experience here on earth. Use it to appreciate the everyday delicacies of existence, and freshen up by feeding your five senses. *What wonders are you worthy of cherishing right now?*

PAGE OF WANDS

PAGE OF CUPS

PAGE OF SWORDS

PAGE OF PENTACLES

* ✷ *

MAGIC TRICK:
Flashcard Feelings

April's energies are all about cutting through the complication and stripping down to the most essential aspects of existence. Tap this bold building block sensation by cycling through all seventy-eight cards of your deck and employing a first thought, best thought approach to the meaning of each. Simply view each card one by one and jot down the stream-of-consciousness notion that surfaces—letting it be as skinny as a single word or phrase. And then play with reading and acting on those primary sensations: pulling a card, recalling your word or phrase, and making a move accordingly.

· →→ 👁 ←← ·

April Tarotscopes

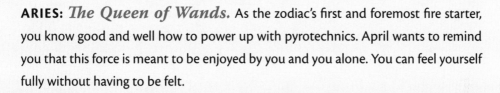

ARIES: *The Queen of Wands.* As the zodiac's first and foremost fire starter, you know good and well how to power up with pyrotechnics. April wants to remind you that this force is meant to be enjoyed by you and you alone. You can feel yourself fully without having to be felt.

TAURUS: *The Emperor.* You relish the sensation of two feet on solid ground, and April wants to give you even more of this luscious land. The Emperor urges you to find the stability you crave by acknowledging the impact your powerful presence makes on every space you enter.

GEMINI: *The Ace of Wands.* As the zodiac's prism, you're forever refracting what's here into more colorful possibilities. April wants you to perform even more of your magic on what presents. Alight on the vitality that catches your attention and then act on it without hesitation.

CANCER: *The Two of Wands.* Sometimes you get caught up in defending your life instead of asserting your right to live it. April wants you to practice stepping into your role as a powerful protagonist. Become an even more courageous creator by pitching before you're asked to do so.

LEO: *The Emperor.* Feeling the effects of your furry force is one of your fave things, and April wants you to hone this power. Relish the responsibility you have to show up and shine on, and beckon each flower face toward your glorious sun with care and consideration.

VIRGO: *The Queen of Wands.* You're a private dancer who glitters and glows brightly in the backroom boudoirs. April invites you to remember that you can

express yourself according to your own integral rhythm, without having to flash your tassels on others' timelines.

LIBRA: *The 3 of Wands.* In your perfect world of all things bright and beautiful, you sometimes want to execute elegantly on your very first go. April invites you to relax your projections about performance and power up by playing in the process instead.

SCORPIO: *The Tower.* One of the zodiac's strongest forces of nature, you have every kind of weather swirling in your corner of the sky. April urges you to relish the force of that storm: let every happening in your wild world become even more fuel for the hurricane that is you.

SAGITTARIUS: *The Ace of Wands.* You're a queenie who's ready for the whole shebang before it's even begun. April is your reminder that you can start small without losing one bit of your bigness. Instead, find enjoyment in watching each moment unfurl like a tiny, tender shoot.

CAPRICORN: *The 4 of Wands.* Forever on the hunt for the next hill to climb, you often find your purpose in extending away from the present and into the grand plan. April wants to remind you that you get to enjoy the effects of all those executions in the right here and right now.

AQUARIUS: *The Tower.* You love to bring it down and bust it out, exhilarating the world into its next big bang. April is here to remind you to notice and respect all the forces at play. Trust that there's more than just you moving and shaking to help create the changes you crave.

PISCES: *The 2 of Wands.* Sometimes you're so enamored with fusion that you forget you're a different phenomenon from the feely fuzz that surrounds you. April is an opportunity to separate and strike out solo. Let yourself be invigorated by this act without it having to feel lonely.

As you depart April's courageous cookout and prepare to let May serve you all of the biscuits your boldness has baked, start to cultivate your own kind of "edible" vision. Whether it's an actual five-course meal, or melodious music on the street, notice how touches, tastes, sounds, and smells can all fill and fuel you, and relish how you absorb their riches.

Now, gather your April and May cards into two separate piles and pluck a pal from each pack. Use April's selection to ensure your aliveness, and May's friend to teach you how to start living well.

L ie back and spread your deck. Pluck each card like a juicy fruit from the vine, drawing its magic to your lips. At May's alfresco feast, your only task is to slip into something more comfortable and take your pleasure with ease . . .

This month's tarot cards bring the buffet right to our boudoir door: *Can you summon the courage to enjoy more of your life?*

MAY

The Magic of Ripeness

In the Stars: May is marinated in the Fixed Earth energy of Taurus. Fixed energy absorbs, and Earth energy sensualizes. Back in January, we met the Earth element through Capricorn's bone-building. This month, Taurus takes its cues from perfumed pleasure planet, Venus; and we're asked to go from Capricorn's up-and-at-'em vertical stance on the earth to Taurus' horizontal roll on it. A tangible way to access what Taurus energy feels like is to watch things get replenished: a soap dispenser being filled; a buffet plate stacked high. In May's land of plenty, getting laden with lusciousness becomes its own form of beauty-baring strength.

In the Cards: May's cardstock is made from harvest-ready hedonism, and each of its six archetypes invites you to fresh-squeeze the juice from each moment—relishing your life's richness all the way to the very last drop without grasping for future fill-ups. These cards represent the earth's spontaneously generating more-ness: here to remind us that we are honeypots who attract the goodies simply by bathing our cells in life's nectars. They are the deck's lotion gloves. Let them smooth any sharp edges of scarcity mentality and ease you into a full-body massage.

In Your Life: To ripen toward May's fruits, you can embrace a **daily practice** of "receiving richness"—noticing how your pores dilate and flower open when you allow yourself to take in a taste, touch, sight, sound, or scent that you treasure; embracing more of what truly fuels you and fills you up; and treating yourself to a little more comfort, even if it's as micro as undoing a top button in a tough moment. In an aggressively prove-it powered world, let May be a radical reminder that you're innately worthy of the good stuff without always having to push. Here not just to live but to live well, May is your month for taking yours right now. And for making it a triple!

At this month's all-inclusive resort, everything is edible. And everything is *for* you. So unfold your petals, lap it up, and lick the spoon.

ZODIAC SIGN: Taurus
ELEMENT: Earth
QUALITY: Fixed
CARDS: the Empress; the Hierophant; the 5/6/7 of Pentacles; the King of Pentacles
MAGIC WORDS: Receiving. Edibility. Fertility. Ampleness. Ease.

≽ MONTH'S DEBUT ≼
MAJOR ARCANA

Take the first few weeks of the month to land in these card landscapes—orienting yourself to their themes and exploring their turf through meditation and visualization. You may also want to return to the inquiry questions as part of your daily practice.

The Empress + The Hierophant

May's pair of Major Arcana deities packs our lunch box with the *food that fuels our vibrancy*—reminding us that we matter enough to decide the menu that makes up our matter. When we pull these cards, or choose to work with them intentionally, we get a snackable sneak peek into what best sustains and supports us: both what we decide to take into our beautiful bods to replenish and enrich us, as well as the embodied beliefs buried in our storehouses that may be ready for a revamp.

THE EMPRESS: Flower Food

When we step into this card's climate, the feast of life is *on*. Bodacious blooms are busting open. Fruit cocktail cups are overflowing. Honeybees are having at it. All around us, life is making love to itself to make more beautiful babies. As everything around us pinks up, we might blush at the prospect of the Empress' *muchness*. Maybe feeling into the Empress makes us a little shy in the face of it all. Do we really deserve all this? But instead of asking ourselves that question, the Empress reminds us to see its wealth as a reflection of our very own magnetism. We are precious pieces of this erotic exuberance, bringing saturated sensation to every petal. No matter what life moment you find yourself in, this card asks you to make love to as much of it as you're willing to.

Each of us, courtesy of incarnation, has been gifted a lifelong pass to the buffet. And when we arrive in this card's energy, we're reminded that we deserve this decadence, as well as the ability to decide how much of it we want to heap onto our plates. **Availability to receive life's more-ness** is made to be custom-crafted and personally designed according to our current appetites and attitudes. How much do we have room for right now? Sometimes, we're bottomlessly hungry,

sopping all of a situation's sweet liqueurs right up. And other times, we're uninterested, unavailable, or unwilling to join the party. Whether these moments of contraction spring from fears of deservedness in the face of life's opulent offerings, or a designated decision to not take in—it doesn't matter. We get to decide the degree of our opening and receive just the right amount of delight.

There is no card in the tarot that's marked with a binary "good" or "bad," and no right way to experience any of their flavors. Whenever we work with this card, the Empress reminds us only that there's a feast before us. That there's food and fullness on offer, and a place card at the table with our name on it. But we can always choose whether or not to take our seat and dig in. Communing with our capacity for capaciousness doesn't have to feel confrontational. Whatever our capacity, this card wants us to feel good about what we're available to have at and to hold. After all, says the Empress, the pleasure is all ours for the taking.

 TURF TIP Explore the Empress through landscapes that are flush and fertile feasts for the senses. Think tropical gardens, bottomless brunches, superstores, and all-inclusive resorts.

ASK YOURSELF:

What's the sensory inventory of my situation—what touches, tastes, sounds, sights, and scents is this moment offering up?

How much of what's on offer am I available to take in right now?

What is my degree of openness, and where are my limits within that?

Without force-feeding myself, can I take in just a bit more?

What's my relationship to moments of "more-ness"?

What would just feel good right now, pure and simple?

_____

_____

_____

_____

_____

_____

_____

_____

_____

_____

_____

_____

_____

_____

_____

THE HIEROPHANT: You Are What You Eat

THE HIEROPHANT

Stepping into this card's climate can feel layered. You'll see thick stacks of archival materials here. Appetites you've amassed through the ages. Well-seasoned sensations, and stories that have become the stuff of legend. The Hierophant is where habit patterns that have stuck to our bones are stockpiled. When we enter this card, we are confronted with all the hard-earned and battle-hardened stuff that we believe comprises the whole of our being. It represents where all our life experiences have "landed" within us; and how they continue to manifest through our ongoing reactions to the people, places, and situations we encounter. With visual iconography that often features a teacher and their students, this card's habitat houses all of the embodied knowledge we've absorbed from our experiences and emotions. The Hierophant is a living library that holds it all.

Whenever we work with this card, we can start by exploring what we've been holding within ourselves. This can begin super tangibly, with an assessment of our physical storage sites. The marks on our skin. The areas of tautness and looseness in our muscles. Treating this map of our body like the map of our known world, we can ask: What lies where? How does it respond when provoked? What purpose has it served historically, and does it still serve? Taking a simple sensorial spin through the flesh and blood rooms of our bodies lets us see where we've buried bits that might be operating beyond our consciousness. We can then make a conscious choice about whether or not we want to keep bringing this belief system to life again and again. The Hierophant is an opportunity to unearth what's stuck and consider what we want to keep on sticking to.

Anytime we work with this card, we're being asked to look through the storage unit that holds our life story and identify what's been retained: that might include things we've heard, been told, felt, and experienced. Do we really need to keep all this on hand in the name of some anticipated apocalypse? Our beliefs about who we are and what life's all about are only able to take hold when we make space for them in our consciousness. But so many of them are thick with dust, not handled and interrogated since we first digested them as we were coming into being—in childhood, in the womb, or even before this life. And it's here in the Hierophant where we're asked to assess all these muscle memories and gut go-tos. We are what we are and there's certainly material within us that's immutable. But we are also what we've been eating. And the Hierophant wants us to continue to swallow only the most sustaining of snacks.

 TURF TIP Explore the Hierophant through landscapes where material collects and is absorbed. Think storm cellars, stocked pantries, archives, and gut microbiomes.

What matter am I made of? What have I absorbed from my life experiences, and where have I stored it within me?

Which experiences and beliefs are buried deepest, and what purpose do they serve?

What reactions and responses are mere reactivity, and which are evidence of my personal truth?

Which of my habit patterns and belief systems continue to give me strength and solace, and which no longer sustain me?

_____
_____
_____
_____
_____
_____
_____
_____
_____
_____
_____
_____
_____
_____
_____
_____
_____

THE MINOR ARCANA

After exploring the big old biospheres of the Majors, you're ready to get nitty-gritty with the on-the-ground teachings of the Minors. Let the next few weeks of the month feel like a living laboratory as you practice responding to these cards by taking direct action and noticing how they show up in your everyday life.

The 5, 6, and 7 of Pentacles: FILL 'ER UP

As we learn to feast on the Empress and the Hierophant's most nectarous nibbles, we can look to this trio of Minor Arcana card kiddies to transport us to a land of milk and honey that is wholly self-replenishing. Think of these cards as *your self-renewing subscription services*—use each card to treat yourself as your own sustainable source of plenty. As you meditate on their energies, invite in the sensation of feeling endlessly full, no matter how much the outside world is serving up.

THE 5 OF PENTACLES

One of the most corseted of all the tarot's taut-laced 5s, we might arrive in the 5 of Pentacles' energy feeling barren. This card can leave us wanting: afraid we won't get the vital nourishment we're so badly craving. But rather than a sign of future scarcity, this 5's energy is a chance to explore our fundamental right to feel full, regardless of what is or isn't already in our possession. While we might not have everything we believe we need right now, we can nourish ourselves with the belief that we're worthy of it—and turn toward sources of sustenance that are already here.

What am I feeling desperate for in this moment, and who or what do I believe will be the "source" that fills me up?

_____

_____

_____

_____

_____

_____

_____

_____

_____

_____

_____

Tarot To-Do: Engage the concept of emptying and hungering in a playful way. Find some delight in squeezing the last bits out of a tube of lotion. Drain your beverage of choice down to the last drop. Let an exuberant laugh or a smile fall out of you fully and extinguish itself. All of life is filling and emptying in its own time, all the time. Explore how you might find a sense of serenity in these sensations of exhale.

THE 6 OF PENTACLES

Like all of the sweet-scented 6s in the tarot, this card wants us to welcome the give-and-take of its element. And in the Pentacles suit, it's all about the in-out of earthly exchange. Sometimes we've got all the goodies to give, with more than enough to go around. But sometimes, we've got to get more goodies to get good in ourselves—building our own strength back up before we give back out. This 6 helps us notice life's levels of giving and receiving, and lets them self-regulate without scrambling or trying to keep score.

What have I got to give right now, and what do I need to get?

_____

_____

_____

_____

_____

_____

_____

_____

_____

_____

Tarot To-Do: Plan an imaginary, or real, dinner party with a few trusted beloveds. Explore the items you're able to bring in this moment, and what you'd request that someone else offer up. These might be literal dishes, or emotional offerings. Sometimes, we're able to cook a slow roast all day long; and sometimes we need to just drop by the store for a ready-made sheet cake. Practice assessing your energetic needs from a practical place, stripped of self-judgment.

THE 7 OF PENTACLES

Each 7 asks us to investigate our expectations, and in the Earth element we're asked to deepen our self-worth by releasing the pressure of restrictive time limits. Maybe our rush for a quick fix or magical solution in a situation hides fears about finite chances beneath it. Or a belief that duration equals worthiness leaves us feeling unworthy about projects or partnerships that have ended—as if their finite life span is somehow incriminating evidence of our failure. This card asks us to soften both the forced speed-ups and slow-downs, and move to a more personal rhythm of ripening.

How can surrendering my stopwatch help stabilize my sense of self-worth?

_____

_____

_____

_____

_____

_____

_____

_____

_____

Tarot To-Do: Take a day, or portion of a day, to engage in activities without watching the clock. Start to develop your own sense of how long you're willing and able to participate in a particular pursuit. Maybe dinner merits three hours, and responding to emails only fifteen minutes. Rather than pre-planning and blocking segments, let your inner sense shape the unfolding.

THE COURT CARDS

Having acclimatized to the Majors' themes and lived out the Minors' on-the-ground energies, you're now ready to try the Court Cards on for size. Let the final few weeks of the month inspire an identity exploration: using the four "styles" sketched below to see how you're channeling this card's archetype, and/or adding your own way of embodying it to the list.

The King of Pentacles: GET COMFORTABLE

Each of the tarot's King cards is a giant-sized footprint that marks our mega-ness in the world at large. In the Pentacles, we commit to claiming our right to environmental ease. This card teaches us to treat this world as if it were our living room—settling into our favorite chair with our snacks close by, and letting life gather at our feet as we enjoy the show from a secure spot.

We can look to this King whenever we feel like we're chafing against something that is happening—whether it's friction in a relationship or work collaboration; or anything in our lives that makes us feel like we have to contort our core self to fit the context. The King of Pentacles is counter to that feeling of getting strong-armed out of the room, or scrambling to find some scrap of security in a tenuous situation. When we draw support from this card, we can let life respond to us instead of rushing to change ourselves for it: becoming courageously comfy beings who can settle into any room because we *are* the room.

Tap this King to relax into your life—sampling the styles below to see how you might create more at-home-ness in your world.

How can you be more at ease?

_____

_____

_____

_____

_____

_____

KING OF PENTACLES

BREEZEWAYS. Look around your life and see where you could allow for more space and breath. Maybe what you need is a pause in your schedule, or a respite from having to respond to something right away. Experiment with creating literal openings in your living space, like spending time next to an open window, or hanging out on a stoop or porch.

DELUXE SUITE. Look around your life and see where you could allow for more richness and silkiness. Maybe what you need is a reminder of the high quality of your life and your worthiness within it. Without having to blow your budget, see how you might make your space a little more luxe—adding a dimmer switch or a gilded picture frame to the mix.

KIDDIE PROOFING. Look around your life and see which hard edges want to be sanded and Bubble Wrapped. Maybe what you need is some more protection and padding to help you handle life's piercing parts. Imagine you're child-proofing your house for a new small visitor, and notice what you could provide to make it feel safer to navigate.

STILL LIFE. Look around your life and see where you'd like to invite in more *signs* of life. Maybe you feel like you've stagnated, or are caught up in endless struggle without much yield. Whether it's a window box garden, a home aquarium, or a hanging fruit basket, see where you could bring in more biodynamic bounty.

Five-Course Banquet Spread

....

May is our opportunity to relax into leisure time without having to prove our place in the pent-house. Let this spread be a reminder that tarot isn't just about self-inquiry and self-growth—but is also about enjoyment. Like a well-stocked cabinet, your deck is here to offer up the nourishment you need, when you need it.

Start by turning all of your cards faceup and looking at their landscapes the same way you would a case of delectable cakes. Which cards look the most appetizing? Which of these life-worlds would just feel good to step into right now, no questions asked or explanations given?

You will self-select this spread, choosing your five cards consciously, rather than having them "choose you" by flipping them over. Notice what this might activate within your system. Do you feel like the cards' meanings are less real or true because you picked them? Do you feel like they're less potent because they feel pleasurable? Let any uncomfy feelings just be, and practice being with the beauty of whatever cards you've chosen from the case.

*Card 1: **Amuse-bouche.*** Choose this card to set the tone. Which tarot archetype feels like it most inspires you, and just feels fun and free when you see it?

*Card 2: **Appetizer.*** Choose this card to start the party and kick-start the conversation. Which tarot archetype represents the part of you that you'd like to share more with others?

*Card 3: **Salad.*** Choose this card to palate cleanse. Which tarot archetype would help you freshen up and open toward the greenness of new growth right now?

*Card 4: **Entrée.*** Choose this card to find your fullness. Which tarot archetype do you want to have take up most of the precious space on your plate?

*Card 5: **Dessert.*** Choose this card as your bonus bit of sweetness. Which tarot archetype would you really like to have at your table right now, even if you feel like it's "extra"?

Magic Trick:
The Best Stuff on Earth

While the tarot's seventy-eight tastes are definitely here to help us learn how to be with the full human experience, much of May's magic is derived from delighting in our right to deserve what's most delectable. Building on the self-chosen bounty of the spread on the previous page, commit to creating more ease by taking your seventy-eight cards out and choosing to remove the ones you don't want to see right now. It doesn't matter why you don't like them or why they activate your system in some way. Don't even inquire. Just put them away, and let yourself take your pleasure by pulling from whatever delicacies remain in the deck—trusting in your right to want what you want, and to feel good with what you've got on hand.

May Tarotscopes

TAURUS: *The Hierophant.* You've got a penchant for holding—and sometimes burying—life's treasures deep within yourself. May is your chance to take stock of what's been stored. Unearth and investigate all the precious intel that's been packed into your heart over time.

GEMINI: *The 6 of Pentacles.* You're one of the zodiac's careful calibrators, who's here to divine just the right recipe of input and output. May's energies offer up an opportunity to let this nervous system regulation feel oh so natural. Take what you need and give what you've got instinctually.

CANCER: *The 5 of Pentacles.* You're here to trust in the constant conch shell calls of your own heart. Let May remind you that no one outside of you can give or take away your solid ground. As the tides ebb and flow, know that you can always serve as your own source of nourishment.

LEO: *The 7 of Pentacles.* You eagerly reach for once-in-a-lifetime moments, riding the roller coaster of sensation like a joyous kiddo. Let May remind you that pleasure can also come in a drama-free drip. Appreciate each morsel without having to chase down the hedonistic highs.

VIRGO: *The 5 of Pentacles.* In your hunt to hone your craft, you sometimes apprentice yourself to outside authority and forget your own. May is here to remind you that you can be your own source of sweetness: a petaled powerhouse who brings all the bees to the yard.

LIBRA: *The King of Pentacles.* Your aspirational energies are perpetually stretching toward the luminous heights. May wants to remind you that you also have the right to embrace what just comes easy. Find elegance in what occurs naturally instead of breaking your back to better yourself.

SCORPIO: *The Empress.* You're the cosmos' greatest composter. You clip the excess from life and throw it in the bin with celestial precision. Amidst all this cutting out, May is here to remind you about fullness. Before you smooch anything goodbye, practice holding it close while it's still here.

SAGITTARIUS: *The Hierophant.* As a wide-eyed wanderer perpetually looking for the truths of existence, you're prone to fall head over heels for "out there" explanations. May is here to remind you that you can also mine your own accumulated experience for the wild wisdom you crave.

CAPRICORN: *The 7 of Pentacles.* You're a five-year planner who understands that the house of dreams is built brick by brick over time. May wants you to take some time off from this countdown. For a change, surrender to inner rhythms and sensuous cycles that don't keep to the clock.

AQUARIUS: *The King of Pentacles.* You're one of the zodiac's premier space holders, here to embrace the diversity of life. Let May remind you of this power to create comfortable contexts for yourself and others to express within, and welcome a greater range of life into your rooms.

PISCES: *The Empress.* A shape-shifter who embraces a liminal existence, you're a lover of life's formlessness. May is an invitation to trust the feedback that comes from touching in with more of the tangible. Immerse yourself in the five senses before you evanesce into the sixth.

ARIES: *The 6 of Pentacles.* Forever upright and at it, your energy often outputs without a second thought about building it back up. May is your moment to consider the courage that can come from receiving. Let lapping up life-force with ease be as vital as going hard at potential challenges.

*A*s you depart May's saturated land of having and holding and head for June's taste-the-rainbow possibilities, explore "butterfly effects." Each entity that moves through the world affects it, and you are part of this life-changing conversation. A few sweet words to a stranger that inspire. A small gesture that shifts the course. There is no magic making that is too micro.

Now, gather your May and June cards into two separate piles and pluck a pal from each pack. Let May's card represent your here-to-stay source of stability. And invite June's card to be your ethereal escort—here to take you by the hand and walk beside you for a little while.

Let each card in your deck alight on your fingertips. Receive their magic messages like winged love letters, leaving their trace as they're translated through you. In June's porous prism, all of life is leading elsewhere . . .

This month's tarot cards inhale and exhale: *What will you become with your next breath?*

JUNE

The Magic of Breath

In the Stars: June is color-changed by the Mutable Air energy of Gemini. Mutable energy adapts, and Air energy respires. Back in February, we met Air through Aquarius' panoramic width. This month, Gemini answers to messenger planet Mercury's mood ring; and we're invited to shift from Aquarius' Fixed vault of the sky to Gemini's buoyant breezes. A tangible way to access what Gemini energy feels like is to witness things getting lifted and led: birds transporting threads for the nest; a paper bag spirited down the street; a beloved beckoning you onto the dance floor. In June's kaleidoscope, possibilities spring to life when we let ourselves lighten up.

In the Cards: June's cardstock is made from sliding door serendipities, and each of its six archetypes invites you to reprise your role as a companion and channel for the universe—rising to meet whatever messages arrive and translating them through your own tongue. These cards represent life's invisible threads and breadcrumb trails: here to take us across thresholds and show us signs. They are the deck's escorts. Let them both send you on your own way and help you become a way-finder for others, changing the course of lives through just one wink and arm link.

In Your Life: To morph toward more of June's magic, you can embrace a **daily practice** of "meeting the multitudes"—noticing the here-for-now and gone-in-an-instant variety of moods, thoughts, actions, and roles you take on, even in the course of a single day; and letting curiosity about these shifts help you better adapt to external fluctuations. You never know who you might be for this world. And who and what within it might be "for" you. A reminder that all of life is forever pollinating and exchanging, June wants you to become a mini bazaar of humanity where all sorts of treasures are traded.

In this month's whisper-down-the-lane land of levitation, secret admirers are waiting in the wings to help you on your way. Let your touch be light as you buzz between ways of being, dancing to meet each changing melody with sneakered feet.

ZODIAC SIGN: Gemini
ELEMENT: Air
QUALITY: Mutable
CARDS: the Magician; the Lovers; the 8/9/10 of Swords; the Knight of Swords
MAGIC WORDS: Prism. Exchange. Channeling. Adaptation. Metamorphosis.

MAJOR ARCANA

Take the first few weeks of the month to land in these card landscapes—orienting yourself to their themes and exploring their turf through meditation and visualization. You may also want to return to the inquiry questions as part of your daily practice.

The Magician + The Lovers

June's double dip of Major Arcana deities is an invite to step outside and into the swirl—two *party-packed spinning piñatas* that ask us to welcome life's unexpected and let it metamorph us into new forms. When we pull these cards, or choose to work with them intentionally, we learn the art of reciprocity: perfectly positioned to understand both our own effect, and the external world's effect on us; and to actively participate in the energetic exchanges that are always abuzz all around us.

THE MAGICIAN: Antenna Up

Stepping into this card's climate asks us to send out a flare so more of life can find us. There's something alive in the air. Something coming. Something already here and buzzing into becoming. Like Christmas Eve, or the much-desired package on the way, an inspiration is reaching out and seeking to reach us. One of the subtlest sensations in the whole of the deck, the Magician asks us **to remain available for the interception**: creating whatever pores are possible to meet life's messages in a given moment, and to answer them back.

We hear a lot of talk about creative "channeling," and it can sound super sexy—conjuring images of artists who seem above the world, letting the baby butterflies of inspiration just alight on their shoulders to bring beautiful concepts to life. But the reality of any creative process is considerably more complex, and asks us to attune to our own balance between wielding inspiration and "working" it as we push our dreams out onto the canvas; and knowing when to hollow ourselves to let the work work through us. We don't have to be self-identified artists to co-mingle with this card's energy, though. We need only remember that all of us are constantly creating our lives: intercepting little lightning bolts of ideas, charging them with our passion and ability,

I

THE MAGICIAN

and then sending them back out into the world, changed, all the time. Whether we're mixing up a mean marinara for suppertime, or bringing a full-blown bestseller into being, how will we participate in life's creative conversations?

Each one of us reads the world and translates it through a different tongue—speaking our life language with particular intonations and accents. And creation, god, the unseen world—whatever you want to call it—wants to bring certain bits through us and only us. Visuals of this card often depict a figure with one arm antenna-up toward the heavens, magic wand in hand, while the other touches down to earth. Whenever we work with the Magician, we're asked to consider the way we tune our voices to call out for inspiration, and holler back our creations into concrete. Maybe we're a screamer who yells at the sky in splashy tones, and then hurls back autographed murals big enough to canvas the world. Or maybe we're a quiet creator who awaits inspiration's soft landing with palms up, and then leaves our unsigned offering on the doorstep, Secret Santa style. No matter how we participate, this card wants us to notice how we open up to what wants to open toward us.

Getting curious about how inspiration arrives and how we respond to it reminds us that life's most creative conversations happen when we make room for a pause in the exchange. Keeping a piece you've penned untitled for the moment, until the right name arrives. Allowing dinner to go unplanned until a strong appetite strikes. Keeping a relationship undefined so its true purpose can emerge. Leaving space lets our lives become more breathable. And in this space, even more inspo can naturally find us. A call to consider the liminal wherever it lives, the Magician wants us to look alive to the adaptable within us. And like jazz musicians just riffing, or chefs whipping up a snack with whatever's on hand, we bring through what already wants to be brought through us and us alone.

 TURF TIP Explore the Magician through landscapes that are poised to intercept the arrival of magic. Think mailboxes, blank pages, altars with offerings, and lighted porches and lobbies.

ASK YOURSELF:

What's hanging in the air right now that I'm starting to sense?

How can I add space to my life to let inspiration in?

What inspires me, and how does inspiration come through my channel?

What's my relationship with the in-between, and how do I use it to adapt to life?

How does life speak to me, and how do I talk back?

What is my current balance between input and output, and how can I calibrate this to best serve my system?

_____

_____

_____

_____

_____

_____

_____

_____

_____

_____

_____

_____

_____

_____

_____

THE LOVERS: The DJ and the Dancer

This card's biosphere is akin to a busy city intersection packed with almost-invisible, nearly missed connections; or a field abuzz with bugs rubbing their legs in chorus—each a vital piece of the meadow's subtle symphony. When we fully immerse ourselves in the Lovers' mix, all of existence wiggles in harmony around us. And we're invited to remember that we're just as much a part of this magic as every other particle that's moving and grooving out there along with us.

Whenever we work with this card, we can return to this month's theme of ethereal escorts. The Lovers asks us to consider how we usher those around us across their thresholds, with or without conscious knowledge of our impact on their lives; and how we are ushered in turn, buoyed by all the little helpers waiting in the wings to carry us through our own crossings. When we pluck the Lovers from our decks, its meaning doesn't have to be attached to any kind of romantic love affair at all. Instead, we're simply being called to consider **the mutuality and reciprocity in our given situation** or life moment. Maybe we've been reaching out in a particular relationship—or longing to come into one—and we've given ourselves over completely to what that real or imagined person supposedly symbolizes in our lives. Or we've been wishing and hoping to duet with a dreamy plan or project so deeply that we feel its gorgeousness is outside of us to be "gotten"—forgetting that our own hoping for it reflects back to us the already-present part that we seek.

Every time we look at life with the eyes of love, it looks right back, awakened by our own ability to see it. And in the Lovers' landscape, we're reminded that we're always both the guided and the guide, the lover and the beloved. We have the ability to lead people and situations just as much as we long to take their lead. Both a boomerang back to our own being, and a message in a bottle tossed into the whipping waves of want, the Lovers' energy is the DJ *and* the dancer—a state of mutual attraction that underlines all of life. When we realize that this exchange and duality is happening inside us all the time, we stop seeing the either/or in the world at large. This knowledge helps us come into communion with our own lovability. There is no need to seek out the supposedly missing bits: it's all there. When we know this, it's easier to get curious about life, and to partner with the energies that meet us exactly where we are.

 TURF TIP Explore the Lovers through landscapes that promote divine dialogue. Think message boards, urban intersections, mutual interest meet-ups, and dance floors.

ASK YOURSELF:

What am I seeking to partner with in the world and why?

Where might this energy I seek also already exist within me?

In my current situation or life moment, who or what is helping guide me, and who or what am I helping to guide?

What have I given away or given over that's ready to be boomeranged back?

What would a more reciprocal exchange with life look like right now?

_____

_____

_____

_____

_____

_____

_____

_____

_____

_____

_____

_____

_____

_____

_____

_____

_____

_____

THE MINOR ARCANA

After exploring the big old biospheres of the Majors, you're ready to get nitty-gritty with the on-the-ground teachings of the Minors. Let the next few weeks of the month feel like a living laboratory, as you practice responding to these cards by taking direct action, and noticing how they show up in your everyday life.

The 8, 9, and 10 of Swords:
FUNHOUSE MIRRORS

As we channel inspiration from the Magician and the Lovers, we can look to this trio of Minor Arcana cards to show us which of the winged wonders that flit before our eyes are meant to be seen as truth—and which are just passing through on their way elsewhere. Think of these cards as a spin through *the amusement park of your own consciousness.* Use each card to consider all of the psychedelic pleasures and perils at play within your kaleidoscope, and choose which you really want to take for a ride.

THE 8 OF SWORDS

The 8s are always our loop the loops of sliding closer to what's real, and in the consciousness-clearing Swords suit, they honeycomb us open to the possible portals and secret passageways. No experience is ever a complete dead end: each life moment pokes little points into the wall of a new life-world that awaits on the other side. This 8 asks us to get curious about how a seemingly intractable sensation or situation is more porous than we might think is possible.

Where am I feeling trapped and why? What either/ors am I believing?

_____

_____

_____

_____

_____

_____

_____

_____

_____

_____

Tarot To-Do: Pen down all of the black-and-whites and either/ors you've been experiencing. Maybe it's change-or-die stakes you've placed on a relationship. Or a belief that criticism about a project means you have to scrap all your work. Then, take a breath, and start creating "third spaces" between the black-and-whites, sketching out as many alternate possibilities as you can imagine, even if they feel highly unlikely to your conscious mind right now. Just inhabit the posture of these porous spaces, sending your breath into their bundles of becoming.

THE 9 OF SWORDS

Each 9 is a pocket of privacy within its element, and here in the swirling mental sensations of the Swords—a suit that sometimes inspires anxiety as our big old brains spin out—we might find ourselves alone after dark with some of our scariest stories. But these machinations of the mind are only here to show us the depth of our tenderness, and the extent of our inventiveness. A chance to face the fright nights and let them reveal the stuffed animals we want to hold safest, this card's contortionism gifts us the power to take a new, less spine-chilling shape.

When I probe beneath my scariest stories about life, what vulnerabilities can I uncover that want tending?

_____

_____

_____

_____

_____

_____

_____

_____

_____

_____

Tarot To-Do: Go ahead and play out all your worst-case scenarios, giving voice to the furry frights that have been lurking under the bed. After you've played out these scaries to their most super sized, create a little spaciousness within them. This might come from laughing at how silly they now seem. Or—if they still feel quite serious—exploring what fear or longing lives beneath them, then penning a list of resources you might need to face these fears.

THE 10 OF SWORDS

Each tarot 10 is a grand finale of its element, and in the Swords, we're gifted our patents as world-class inventors. What if all the stories you told yourself—from the scary ones that keep you cowering to the epic adventures of greatness—were actually just proof of your own ingenuity? This card wants you to claim your role as an imaginative being: shifting your creative energy away from half-truths and toward supportive stories; blowing your own mind by getting out of your head entirely.

If I gave all my stories a truth serum right now, what would they tell me? Where am I being asked to get out of my head and connect with a larger truth?

_____

_____

_____

_____

_____

_____

_____

Tarot To-Do: Play a variation of the game "two truths and a lie" with yourself. Let the lie be a statement that makes you feel small and that you no longer have use for. And let the two truths be both true and aspirational—stories you want to give even more energy. For example, the "lie" might be: "I always magnetize painful partnerships." And the truths might be: "I've learned a lot about my emotional resilience through my relationships" and "I am open to welcoming in a new love story." Speak each of these aloud and notice how each is received by your body, listening to your voice and noticing your breath. Then, start to turn down the volume on the lie—whispering it until it disappears. Plump the other two statements up, shouting them to the winds. Then, take one action, however small, that supports each of these two truthy truths.

THE COURT CARDS

Having acclimatized to the Majors' themes and lived out the Minors' on-the-ground energies, you're now ready to try the Court Cards on for size. Let the final few weeks of the month inspire an identity exploration: using the four "styles" sketched below to see how you're channeling this card's archetype, and/or adding your own way of embodying it to the list.

The Knight of Swords: EXPLORE YOUR OPTIONS

Each Knight is our spirit's guide to inhabiting the in-between—here to help us limbo with all of life's liminality. In the Air element, we're asked to get lighter and looser on our feet, leaning on our ability to skim the surface and quicken our step so we can color-change through the constant changes.

We all have different penchants for adapting our approach and sampling more of life's possibilities: some of us find flexibility all too easy, lava lamping our way through life; while others of us clench our toes at the slightest flutter of change. This Knight asks us to explore our natural wiring on this shape-shifting spectrum—remaining nimble enough to meet the magic of "maybe" without polarizing into all-out amorphousness, or bolted-to-the-ground entrenchment.

Tap this Knight by adopting your own style of aerated adaptability—seeing which of the winged wonders below you want to channel to help give you a lift.

How could you lighten up your life?

_____

_____

_____

_____

_____

_____

KNIGHT OF SWORDS

BUTTERFLY WINGS. Maybe you feel ready to curiously sample alternatives—uncovering options by opening yourself to new creative combos. Try on this levitation technique by taking tiny tastes from many of life's flowers. Expose yourself to a greater range of opinions, expressions, and experiences.

LIGHT AS A FEATHER. Maybe you feel ready to connect with life's mystical mood ring—uncovering options by becoming intimate with the subtle mysteries of change. Try this levitation technique by noticing inexplicable serendipities and chance encounters. Open yourself to surprise happenings without seeking to overexplain.

BOUNCY CASTLE. Maybe you feel ready to embrace life's effervescent "what-ifs"—uncovering options by delighting in the always-evolving adventure. Try this levitation technique by seeking out moments of "maybe" and leaving parts of your life as-of-yet undefined. Jiggle with life's jumpies and embrace the excitement of change.

LIGHTHOUSE. Maybe you're in need of some safety in the face of shape-shifting—finding the courage to uncover options by first firming up your footing. Try this levitation technique by creating some fortifications in the flux. Anchor yourself in stable truths and known quantities, and then start to notice what's wiggling on the horizon.

Cocktail Conversation Spread

....

As you build your mix-and-match muscles this month, the spread below can help you feel into your deck's internal conversations, and make peace with the both/and elements of your life moment.

Pull three pairs of cards and follow the prompts below. Then, imagine you were at a cocktail party, as your question circulates between these pairs. Listen in for each card pair's "take" on your situation, and notice how their unique perspective will arise through a customized blend of the two individual cards' respective meanings. How might the after-dark scaries of the 9 of Swords face the Empress' bloom-laden bounty as they discuss your fears about a relationship ending? What would the Tower's all-mighty forces say to the 7 of Pentacles' steady sense of self-worth vis-à-vis your desire to take on more responsibility at work? Practice holding both card meanings contemporaneously, as you do the same within your situation. If you get stuck, draw inspiration from the visuals—imagining the elements of one picture entering the space of the other and co-mingling.

*Card Duet 1: **The Tried-and-Trues.*** These two cards are true-blue friends who stick together no matter the situation. Their conversation symbolizes the heart of your situation—the themes that want to forgo the small talk and get right to the good stuff, talking all night if necessary to reach the root of the issue. Imagine what these two cards would say to each other if they held nothing back, and imagine their intense tête-à-tête forming the center of this chatty cocktail party.

*Card Duet 2: **The Frenemies.*** This pair of cards symbolizes the uncomfortable aspects of your situation—the dueling questions that are creating sparks as they conflict with each other. But it's a love-hate relationship: their friction drives each card forward to greater meaning. Imagine how these two energies could broker a deal within you, learning to live and let live on each other's alternating sides.

*Card Duet 3: **The New Lovers.*** At this party, the cards are all gossiping about your question, and this pair symbolizes its hidden potential. You may not know it yet, but these are the elements that could be unexpectedly combined to create a portal of possibility. Imagine how these two energies might catalyze a third way, blending their two meanings into a new path forward.

* ✳ *

MAGIC TRICK:
Taste the Rainbow

June is the perfect time to practice double- and triple-dipping all the flavors of the tarot by learning to live through the whole of your deck. Take all seventy-eight cards out and travel through them at whatever your pace, pulling out each one and reading about their respective meanings (you'll find a card-by-card mini reference in the back of this book, which is a good place to start). You can do this in a variety of ways: you might pick a different card to work with each day for seventy-eight days; or a different one each hour, or even minute, for a more moment-by-moment ride. You might even consciously pull every card, one at a time, in response to a single question: answering it seventy-eight different ways, and using this practice as a reminder that no feeling is ever final or fated. Notice the sensations that swirl within you as you sift through this rainbow of emotion, trying on each card for size and then moving on as the spirit moves you.

· →→ 👁 ←← ·

June Tarotscopes

GEMINI: *The 10 of Swords.* Sometimes your sushi-belt style of living can get dizzying, as you reach out for a nibble of everything that flies by. Let June remind you that this ability to see the options is a mark of resilience. Wield your right to change your mind, and your life, at whim.

CANCER: *The Knight of Swords.* A sweet baby barnacle, finding shelter from life's storms is one of your superpowers. Let June help you ensure that those sanctuaries stay breathable. Allow people, emotions, and situations to pass in and out of your loving lair with greater ease.

LEO: *The Lovers.* Part of your power comes from the mutuality of both looking upon this world with love, and having it look right back at you. June is a chance to commune fully with this duet. Remind yourself that everything you feast your eyes on is also winking your way.

VIRGO: *The 9 of Swords.* A picnic basket of preparedness, you love readying yourself to respond. Let June be a respite from this energy. Conjure the most likely—and most desirable—happenings in your head, and then support those without spreading yourself thin.

LIBRA: *The 10 of Swords.* Always spinning life into just the right light, you're a cutie who knows how to curate. Let June remind you that overhauls can come from places of joy. Embrace exhilaration about future changes, instead of dissatisfaction with the present imperfect.

SCORPIO: *The 9 of Swords.* You're no stranger to what lurks under the floorboards, spelunking beneath to excavate the buried beasts. Let June be your

chance to create portals as you probe. Lift up the rocks and reveal that maybe your worst fears are actually part fantasy.

SAGITTARIUS: *The Magician.* You are a seeker of signs who can make meaning out of even the most mundane of mud piles. June is your chance to reignite your inspiration station. Swap statements for question marks, and surprise yourself by the twists and turns your tale takes as you tell it.

CAPRICORN: *The 8 of Swords.* You know how to handle life's heft with aplomb, taking it all on for the long haul. June wants you to also allow yourself to back out and course-correct as needed. Trust that you can revise the terms of lifelong commitments that are sucking the life right out of you.

AQUARIUS: *The Knight of Swords.* You've got a rep for flying high above the clouds, powered by firm faith in your perspective. Let June be an invite to let your ideas live and learn through trial and error. Test-drive the creative maybe-babies of possibility and stay open to adapting your approach.

PISCES: *The Magician.* You're a séance of a human who is always able to divine the subtlest of signs from the unseen world around you. Let June help you pluck one notion out of the ether and act on it. Balance all that mediumship with the output of a concrete creation.

ARIES: *The Lovers.* As the zodiac's original big banger, you sometimes feel like you're flying solo through this wild world. Let June be your reminder of co-creative acts. Hand out your heat like cinnamon candy, but remember to reach out for a helping hand when you need it.

TAURUS: *The Knight of Swords.* While you relish reliable sources of strength to get you through the day, June wants you to add some pep to your steady step. Remember that your enjoyment of the decadent in life can be even more deluxe when you sample new perspectives from the menu.

As you depart June's prism of possibility and prepare to land in July's homecoming cove, start to notice the protective coverings that keep life safe. The shells of mollusks. The swaddling cloth that wraps an infant. Samosa pockets. Sense into what wants to remain tucked safely within you and imagine gift-wrapping yourself in the kind of casing you feel would envelop you with strength.

Now, gather your June and July cards into two separate piles and pluck a pal from each pack. Harness June's archetype to help keep your existence winged and buoyant, while July's friend shelters you from any storms.

Cover yourself with your deck. Encircle your being within its private cove and follow each card's tidal pull back to shore. Inside July's secret diary, our softest parts are kept safe and sound . . .

This month's tarot cards hold us nearer and dearer, whispering: *What does your heart call home?*

JULY

The Magic of Sanctuary

In the Stars: July is bathed in the Cardinal Water energy of Cancer. Cardinal energy claims, and Water energy surrounds. Back in March, we met Water through Pisces' misty allowing. This month, Cancer charts its course in keeping with the insistent rhythms of its ruling body, the moon itself. We're asked to go from getting carried out into Pisces' ethers, to getting brought back—bundled in beach blankets that pad us with protection. A tangible way to access what Cancer energy feels like is to explore homing devices: apartment lights at dusk drawing dwellers in to dinner; shell shapes echoed to shore. In response to July's lunar magnetics, everything is finding its way inside.

In the Cards: July's cardstock is made from sea-soaked stuff, and each of its seven archetypes is an invite to tend and mend our vulnerable bits and answer our inner calls. These cards remember us: presiding over our emotional lineage and family lines; offering us safe harbor from suffering; and asking us to become proud homeowners of our inner worlds. They are the deck's beach bungalows and seashell purses. Use their locks and clasps to both protect what's precious and to welcome more of your wet and wild emotions within.

In Your Life: To make friends with July's feeling foam, you can embrace a **daily practice** of "heart homecoming"—considering the carrying cases and comfort sources you use to safeguard your most sensitive self; and tracing the emotions you've inherited back to their source—whether springing from families of origin or beyond—so you can decide what you want to continue carrying. Whether you're folded like a delicate dumpling or exposed like a clam on the half shell serving your heart on a platter, July wants to remind you that whatever the shape and state of your heart, you have the right to design its den. Take this month to feel what you feel, let in who you want, and love how you want to love.

Longing. Sadness. Exhilaration. Rage. Forgiveness. Joy. July turns the tub taps on and floods us with feeling. After the skinny-dip, we'll be swaddled to shore, made stronger by softening toward the spumyness of our most untamable tides.

ZODIAC SIGN: Cancer
ELEMENT: Water
QUALITY: Cardinal
CARDS: the High Priestess; the Chariot; the Ace/2/3/4 of Cups; the Queen of Cups
MAGIC WORDS: Incubation. Shelter. Belonging. Protection. Memory.

MAJOR ARCANA

Take the first few weeks of the month to land in these card landscapes—orienting yourself to their themes and exploring their turf through meditation and visualization. You may also want to return to the inquiry questions as part of your daily practice.

The High Priestess + The Chariot

July's duet of Major Arcana deities represents our *shells of self-protection*. They are here to welcome us into the inner sanctums that best support our sensitivity, but also to teach us when the time is right to leave home and move on. When we pull these cards, or choose to work with them intentionally, it's a chance to consider the carapaces that cover and carry us; how we shield ourselves from life's storms and forge an unbreakable bond with our inner wisdom; and how we commit to shedding temporary coping mechanisms when they no longer serve us.

THE HIGH PRIESTESS: The Listening Room

We step into this card's climate wholly alone. There is no map to get here. No cookie crumbs left in our wake. No velvet-roped bodyguards or pin codes to punch in and puncture this place within us. Our High Priestess sanctuary arises soundlessly, taking shape whenever we summon the courage to place our ear up close to the conch shell that shelters the wisdom nestled within.

So many of us long to connect with what we call our intuition, and often imagine it as a territory of eternal surety and alignment. Amidst all the noise of "no," wouldn't it be magical to always, somehow, just *know*? Often depicted as a being who's firmly sandwiched between two pillars, the High Priestess beckons us to step inside and begin this work. But the work we do within this card is an ongoing endeavor that is often undertaken in self-containment and total silence. Whenever we enter its energy, we're asked to listen, first and foremost. And to return, again and again—treading the private path to this sanctuary so often that every cell in our being starts to remember its contours. Here, we start to drop into **the place where we know what we know when and how we know it**. And this realization doesn't necessarily hit immediately. The

THE HIGH PRIESTESS

High Priestess beckons us to settle in and steep ourselves in the messages we receive, sitting pretty until we're ready to interpret their contents.

Committing to uncovering innermost knowledge means learning to caretake the conditions that best support accessing it. Each of our styles of listening to our innermost selves will look different, and will want different forms of tending. For some of us, we've got to follow the lava of molten-hot feelings all the way to the center of our personal geodes. For others, the travels might feel lighter, less fraught, as if the answers simply floated in on a breeze. Stay curious about the contours of your inner self, says the High Priestess. And then concierge those contours for eternity.

Our only call in this card is to take care of what is tidal and timeless within us. The rhythms that keep pulling. The private phone calls that cannot be ignored. The after-midnight communications from our truest selves that echo again and again, whispering: *Do not leave my side. Do not relinquish me.* But no matter what we do, there are no screw-ups here. No complete abandonments. No missed or mixed messages. And absolutely no punishments for not picking up on our intuitive pulls. There's only the necessity to continue returning to our rhythms so they can reveal themselves, and our willingness to let our listening lead the way. Bolstering our ability to be beholden to no one's beat but our own, we beat our way back to the center of our hearts.

 TURF TIP Explore the High Priestess through landscapes that are soundlessly self-contained and energetically sealed. Think train quiet cars, silent nights, closed doors, and secluded islands.

ASK YOURSELF:

What is my relationship to silence? What kind of listener am I?

How do "knowings" arrive within me?

When have I followed intuitive hits in the past, and where have they led me?

When have I pushed down these inner knowings, and why?

What messages are insisting that I tend to them right now, and how am I responding?

What does the most private place within me look like, and how can I support its habitat?

_____

_____

_____

_____

_____

_____

_____

_____

_____

_____

_____

_____

_____

_____

_____

_____

THE CHARIOT: Coming-of-Age

VII

THE CHARIOT

Stepping into this card's climate finds us standing on the shifting sands of life. We feel the familiar between our toes, but something new is drifting in. Departures are underfoot. They could feel epic, or infinitesimally small, but when this card arrives, the tides they are a-changin'. And even if we sink our feet into soaked sand and try to get stuck in our old and familiar ways, the procession of the particles inside of us is inevitable. A graduation from some level of life is always under way.

Whenever we work with this card's energy, **we're being birthed through something**. And, in the process, we're called to consider the armor that covers us and the carriers that convey us through change. Whether we're a clam on the half shell, a locked-up lobster, or some other form of seafood entirely, each of us develops a carapace dividing our softest parts from the hardest parts of life. This month, meditate on the energy of the Chariot to explore the ways in which you seek protection against the elements. What is your availability to fully face change? The Chariot reminds us that while some of this Bubble Wrap might be absolutely essential, other bits of our bundling are like well-worn baby blankets that are more habitual than functional. Playing in this card's climate asks us to discern the difference between protection that is necessary and functional, and extraneous exoskeletons that are blocking our bods from maturing.

Like hermit crabs, we often take our old methods of protection with us as we creep outside of our comfort zones. And this card reminds us that when faced with change, we never have to force ourselves to leave our shell. All Water-sign ruled cards in the tarot (the Moon, the Chariot, Death) are here to softly sand down our resistance to participating in life's cycles and release us into the forever-flux. When we slip into their swirl, we start to give up our notions of forward-and-back progress and surrender to the mystery of time. The Chariot's sloshy tidal rhythm is an invitation to let ourselves embrace the experience of alternately washing out into the waves of change and back onto the shores of comfort—knowing that our maturation process is indeed a process, which is wholly personal and totally non-linear.

Like teens coming into adulthood, each of us matures according to our own pattern and rate of growth. Maybe we need extra assurance to try new things and it's valuable to us to make sure we have a support system as we move on. Or we might need the ritual of a celebratory confetti throw to tell all the world that our tides are changing. Or maybe we just growth spurt straight to the next phase of our life—racing toward a new way to be without a second thought. The Chariot reminds us that there's no right or wrong way to carry ourselves through change. We are the midwives of our own momentum. And soul-deep shifts unfold when we embrace the naturally shedding skin we're already in.

 TURF TIP Explore the Chariot through landscapes that shield life's shifts and celebrate stages of growth. Think conveyor belts, graduation toasts, memory montages, and school drop-off zones.

ASK YOURSELF:

What is the envelope that protects me from the world?

How do I guard my softness against life's harshness?

Which of this padding is still serving my growth, and which of it marks a comfort zone that might bear investigating and updating?

In this moment, am I more exposed to or protected from life?

What new kinds of living are beckoning me—and how can I best hold myself as I move on?

_____

_____

_____

_____

_____

_____

_____

_____

_____

_____

_____

_____

_____

_____

_____

_____

THE MINOR ARCANA

After exploring the big old biospheres of the Majors, you're ready to get nitty-gritty with the on-the-ground teachings of the Minors. Let the next few weeks of the month feel like a living laboratory, as you practice responding to these cards by taking direct action, and noticing how they show up in your everyday life.

The Ace, 2, 3, and 4 of Cups:
SKIN SOFTENING

As we learn to caretake our protective coverings in the High Priestess and the Chariot, we can look to this quartet of Minor Arcana kiddies to tenderize us: tending our soft parts and sending much-needed moisture to the pieces of our hearts that have become calloused from hurt. Think of these cards as *your self-care essentials*—using each card to love up on what's most vulnerable within you, and to strengthen your capacity to love from a place that's safe and sound.

THE ACE OF CUPS

Each Ace is our chance to "turn on" to the element in question, and in the watery Cups suit, we open our taps. This could mean pulling the emotional release valve and power-washing our hearts with all-out oceanic sobs. Or it might be a simpler spritz, where we let sharing a feeling with a friend remind us that we no longer have to hold it all so close to the chest. Whatever our style of sea spray, the Ace of Cups asks us to dip into our swimming pool of sensitivity and start our cleanse.

What taps of emotion want to be turned on in me?

_____

_____

_____

_____

Tarot To-Do: Explore your relationship to water, pure and simple. Do you like getting caught in a rainstorm? Would you rather be seaside, bayside, lakeside, or creek-side? Are you a bath or shower person? What kind of beverages do you want to have pass through your lips: fuzzy bubbles, creamy teas, or bitter tonics? Practice letting just a little more of this element into your life on the daily, and gently investigate your preferences.

THE 2 OF CUPS

Each tarot 2 is a tailoring that invites us to find our fit within its element. In the intimate release of the watery Cups, this card asks us to peer into the reflecting pool and soften some aspect of our self-gaze. Sometimes, it's a call to welcome in a part we feel we've got to fix or force out to become worthy of love. Other times, it's an invite to protect ourselves against a vicious voice inside of us that tears us down. Whatever the hard-edged part of self, this 2 wants us to reach out and tiptoe toward it, look into its eyes, and give it a loving tap.

What pushed-away parts of me want to come closer, and which bullying bits of me might want to be gently pushed away?

_____

_____

_____

_____

_____

Tarot To-Do: Sketch out the parts of self you find stickiest and give them nicknames like "Micromanagerial Bess." If it feels too confrontational to title them in this way, gift them neutral names that aren't your own, like "Suzy" and "Zack." Visualize these newly named parts of yourself as students at a high school prom, leaning up against the walls, rife with insecurity and hoping for a tender touch. If you've named some parts of self that are all-out bullies, you might choose to disinvite them to the party, taking care not to further recriminate yourself for their existence. Then, picture moving just a bit closer to the remaining parts of self, and perhaps even asking them to dance.

THE 3 OF CUPS

In the Water element, the bubblelicious 3 becomes an overflowing bathtub of emotional acceptance. This 3 invites us to soften our aspirations for perfect love and statically serene feeling states, and instead become present for honest intimacy that's ever-changing. Wading into its soapsuds means exploring the current state of our heart and its needs, and letting others do the same. A powerful primer in partnering with ourselves and our beloveds in real time, this card asks us to swap fairy-tale, freeze-framed feelings for the many faces of a real love that's right here.

How can I become more emotionally honest in this moment? What can the present state of my heart teach me about what real love actually looks like for me?

_____

_____

Tarot To-Do: Imagine that your heart is a biosphere, and explore its current environment. Maybe you're healing from a deep hurt and it's become a barren desert. Or perhaps it's flooded with edible flowers like a trip to the tropics. As you imagine the creatures who might reside within it, try letting them into your life, reaching for the qualities they symbolize.

THE 4 OF CUPS

Each of the 4s is a cubicle of self-divined care, and here in the Water element, we're invited to chicken-soup ourselves back to a state of heart health. Like a stay-at-home night where we seek solace in a pore-refining face mask, its energy wants to remind us that we have every right to restore and reset our emotions. By honoring our own particular process of becoming emotionally available—taking our time to decide who and what makes us feel safe to share—we build intimacy that's born from the stable core of our beings, instead of from fear of missing out.

What would help me feel emotionally safe right now? What does my heart need a holiday from?

_____
_____
_____
_____
_____
_____
_____
_____
_____

Tarot To-Do: Plan yourself a private present-wrapping party to restore your heart. Imagine how you would choose to celebrate your right to greater serenity and security. Picture placing your precious heart inside of a protected space. Maybe it's sheltered under the shade of a tree. Or sinking into the grooves of a luxurious leather sofa. Or maybe you'd even choose to lock it safely away in an iron vault. Notice what you need to feel emotionally safe, and then practice inviting these elements into your real-life relationships.

THE COURT CARDS

Having acclimatized to the Majors' themes and lived out the Minors' on-the-ground energies, you're now ready to try the Court Cards on for size. Let the final few weeks of the month inspire an identity exploration: using the four "styles" sketched below to see how you're channeling this card's archetype, and/or adding your own way of embodying it to the list.

The Queen of Cups: KEEP YOUR SECRETS

Much like the High Priestess, all four of the tarot's Queens are connected to intuition. You can think of the High Priestess as the gatekeeper of your heart and soul's hotel, and the Queens as honeymoon suites within it: here to welcome you into different facets of your inner world that exist behind closed doors.

The Water-ruled Queen of Cups gets the suite with the private Jacuzzi—inviting us to seek retreat and self-tend our emotions. That could mean energetically "disappearing" for a moment mid-flow in a meeting to collect yourself; or taking a break from beloveds in favor of a solo sojourn that's for your eyes only. Whatever the mood, this Queen compels us to become our own closest confidantes by holding our hearts close to the chest before we ask others to hold them.

Tap this Queen by slipping into your own emotional hideaway—selecting one of the private styles below to build a stronger relationship with your inner contours.

What secret life am I living?

_____

_____

_____

_____

_____

_____

QUEEN OF CUPS

THE SECRET DIARY. This style of communing with your private life is for you if you're ready to get vividly adolescent—saturating yourself in the high drama of your emotional experiences. Play with tricking your emotions out with special soundtracks; DIYing a private pillow fort; and letting yourself fall fully into the arms of your feelings with all the fun-filled flair of a first crush.

THE MIDNIGHT CONFESSION. This style of communing with your private life is for you if you're ready to experience radical emotional honesty with yourself—holding nothing back and staying up till dawn to dig ever closer. Play with making direct eye contact with complex emotions that surface: calling them by name out loud and cutting them back to their core components.

THE CLOAK-AND-DAGGER. This style of communing with your private life is for you if you're ready to revel in your own intrigue—celebrating the complex power that lives in your most covert places. Play with treating your mysterious moods like you would an espionage expedition, gathering intel and observing your delicious strangeness with soft-footed stealth.

THE PRIVATE TRUST. This style of communing with your private life is for you if you're ready to forge a clear and clean commitment to protecting whatever you want to keep covered. Play with establishing your own "terms of engagement" with your emotions: deciding when, where, and how you'll handle them, and respecting them as a force to be reckoned with when the time is right.

The Striptease Spread

....

The Cancerian energy that infuses July is ruled by the moon itself. As this luminary cycles through its waxing and waning stages each month, it burlesques itself slowly, revealing as much skin in a given moment as it wants to share with the sky. Likewise, we can use July to consider our own sensitive stripteases: both the parts of ourselves we'd like to protect from prying eyes, and the shoulders we're ready to bare.

Use the spread below to explore the art of exposure in your life right now—letting yourself sift through your emotional layers and deciding which you'd like to slip off. You can use it to check in with your general revelation style. Or, you might ask about a specific situation where you find yourself polarizing to one end of the spectrum: for example, rushing to overshare with a new lover; or, at the other end, fearfully guarding a cherished dream from ever seeing the light of day.

You might also enjoy aligning this spread's pulls with the phases of the actual moon: pulling Card 1 during the period between the waning and new moon; Card 2 at the new moon; and Card 3 at the full moon reveal moment.

*Card 1: **Tassels.*** This card represents the self-protection that is happening in your situation. It asks you to examine how you might be hiding a part of yourself away from the world. You can explore which elements of this card's armature feel self-chosen, and which parts might only be providing superficial security that's more fear-based than loving.

*Card 2: **Lingerie.*** This card brings you into greater intimacy with your situation. It shows you where you might be ready to reveal some of your qualities to the world, if only for a moment. Explore which bits you'd like to keep just for yourself, and which parts you can play peekaboo with.

*Card 3: **Nakedness.*** This card represents the bits that are ready to be bared—qualities and energies in your situation that no longer want to be hidden. Know that this doesn't need to happen overnight: you can always choose the rhythm of this revelation, and lean on the more secret layers of Cards 1 and 2 to sustain you as you strip down to your skin.

MAGIC TRICK:
Carrying Cases

July is all about selecting the shells that are best suited to protect our inner processes. Cozy into these coves and caverns by exploring how you'd like to physically carry your deck. This is a perfect exercise if you have multiple decks that you use for different kinds of spiritual inquiry. Some decks might demand to be kept in a sacred spot so they can support walking you through the fire of difficult questions. Others won't mind getting tossed in your bag beside a pack of gum—here to pop out and power up at any moment. There are altar-sized decks fit for exhibiting in your home as high art, and there are teeny-tiny decks perfect for on-the-spot draws. Some love to talk love, while others long to get straight to the soul purpose work. There is no right or wrong way to "protect" your deck and its energies. Just like you and your own life vulnerabilities, your deck only wants to be asked about the gifts it's here to give, and how it would like to be treated.

July Tarotscopes

CANCER: *The High Priestess.* You're a tender and a mender, here to help raise the whole world into the strength of adulthood. Take July to incubate an idea that's solely your own: fully possess your internal rhythms and make an independent decision about when it's time to birth it into being.

LEO: *The 2 of Cups.* You're often enamored of a life lived in full sun that holds nothing back and keeps nothing hidden. Let July be a sweet reminder that you can use that lovable light of yours to connect with any parts of your person that have been left for too long in the shade.

VIRGO: *The Chariot.* You're here to develop an unbreakable integrity, only giving the key to your heart to the holiest causes. Let July be an invite to let this inner loyalty evolve with life: checking your system of self-protection to ensure it matches your adventurous expansions.

LIBRA: *The 2 of Cups.* A duet of dichotomies, you're perpetually peering into the mirror to make sense of the other side. Let July's looking-glass gazes be both compassionate and curious. Each facet that's revealed can help you see more of the wondrous human that is you.

SCORPIO: *The Ace of Cups.* Your status as a Fixed Water sign often takes the form of badass ice blocks. July wants you to melt stuck emotions and find more oceanic flow. Unclench any white-knuckled till-death-do-you-part desires and embrace the fluidity of your sign's element.

SAGITTARIUS: *The Chariot.* Well-accustomed to life's departures, you often find yourself with one hoof out the door. July wants to remind you that each of these

transitions is also a graduation worthy of pomp and circumstance. Take time to trick out your threshold crossings in whatever style suits you.

 CAPRICORN: *The 3 of Cups.* The state of your heart sometimes gets side-stepped in service of what you believe to be worthier causes. But July insists that there's nothing more meritorious of your majesty. Use your characteristic, no-holds-barred honesty to receive whatever emotions arise.

 **AQUARIUS:** *The High Priestess.* A keeper of profound mystery and prophetic visions, you're a safe house for all forms of intuition. Take July to check in to your lair of listening: committing ample time and space to letting your instinctual knowings arise and arrive.

 **PISCES:** *The Queen of Cups.* A wet 'n' wild wonder of wavey sensations within, you inhabit the full flux of feelings in plain sight of the rest of us. Take July to check out from having to expose these emotions—instead, bundle yourself in a fleecy blanket of do-not-disturb, private feels.

 ARIES: *The 4 of Cups.* Fully switched on for the next flame-on, you metabolize experiences on the hyperactive fly. Let July be your invite to actually inquire about how it's all been "landing" for you. Explore the impacts on your system before you reset for another rev.

 TAURUS: *The 3 of Cups.* One of your juiciest gifts is your embrace of the natural and instinctual states of human expression. Take July to celebrate this superpower in matters of the heart. Let relationships evolve as organically as wild plants, without attempting to prune them into perfect forms.

 **GEMINI:** *The Queen of Cups.* As life swirls through your open doors, you become a medium for all sorts of sensitivities. July asks you to temporarily close up shop to callers and get curious about the calls that come from within. Let this deep dialogue with yourself reveal secret sources of creative inspo.

As you leave July's shaded lair of inner longings for August's high-noon sparkle and strut, start to explore how things around you expose more essence. How you slip out of a cardigan as the temps heat up. How a juicy fruit loosens its peel and generously drips with just one bite. See how you can bare more skin and shed more layers in the name of love.

Now, gather your July and August cards into two separate piles and pluck a pal from each pack. Let July's pick be your under-the-blouse locket that's held for your heart only, and August's selection be your heart-on-your-sleeve calling card, here for the whole world to feel.

Come closer to your deck, exactly as you are. Show yourself to the entire spread and let it shine back. Sporting a hot pink heart on its sleeve and asking only for yours in return, August simply cannot do without *you* . . .

This month's tarot cards coax us out into the full sun of life's largeness: *Whatever you love, love it louder.*

AUGUST

The Magic of Romance

In the Stars: August is bedazzled by the Fixed Fire energy of Leo. Fixed energy holds more, and Fire energy expresses. Back in April, we met Fire through Aries' fundamental aliveness. This month, Leo answers to the sun's full-spectrum splendor—the celestial body that sits at the center of it all—and we're asked to go from Aries' pulse check to Leo's heartbeat, enlarging our life-force through the eyes of love. A tangible way to access what Leo energy feels like is through adoration: gifting a compliment freely and watching it shower you both in sparkle; experiencing a fond nuzzle from a treasured pet; even flirting with glossy supermarket fruits that are equally ready for your pluck. In August's energy, you are the protagonist in a grand romance—turning each tiny flower face toward the warmth of your willingness to come forward.

In the Cards: August's cardstock is made from fully fluffed stuff, and each of its six archetypes is a leopard-print love-up that lifts us into larger-than-life leotards: here to remind us of the epic feats that are possible when we share more of ourselves. These cards reveal that when we come heart-first and freely, each furry friend can do the same: turning the world into a mutual adoration celebration where seeing and being seen in the light of love gives all of us more life. They are the deck's roll calls. Show up to them in your signature style: giving them your whole heart and getting your glow right back in return.

In Your Life: To bask in August's radiance, you can embrace a **daily practice** of "romantic gestures": saying "I love you" or "I'm sorry" first, without the guarantee that you're going to get it back; beholding yourself and others like you would a new lover, without seeking to adjust a single precious curl on your magic mane; and immortalizing this singular spin round the sun by elevating your everyday existence to epic status. In a world often overwhelmed by gray sameness, this month reminds us that even doing the dishes deserves a bedazzler. Like a glitter kitten leaving your signature scent on the furniture, August wants you to transform every speck of dust around you into a potential piece of flair.

ZODIAC SIGN: Leo
ELEMENT: Fire
QUALITY: Fixed
CARDS: Strength; the Sun; the 5/6/7 of Wands; the King of Wands
MAGIC WORDS: Presence. Play. Exposure. Glow. Specialness.

MAJOR ARCANA

Take the first few weeks of the month to land in these card landscapes—orienting yourself to their themes and exploring their turf through meditation and visualization. You may also want to return to the inquiry questions as part of your daily practice.

Strength + The Sun

August's pair of Major Arcana deities represent *bare beauty*: they're here to help us get comfortable with increased exposure and participate more fully in life. When we pull these cards, or choose to work with them intentionally, it's a chance to simplify our skin-on-skin contact with existence and come into greater presence. Strength and the Sun ask us to enter experiences without armature and to uncover the heart, shedding layers of self-assessment and giving ourselves over to the moment. This month, use these cards to practice showing up, sharing more, and letting each element of your life show itself exactly as it is.

STRENGTH: The Power of Love

We step into this card's climate on a humid Hawaiian night, where our sweatshirt cover-ups are better off left back in the bungalow. The tiki torches are upright and blazing. Marshmallows are softening from their sticks over the bonfire flames. And all the beasties are unabashedly singing their songs, their presence pulsing in the trees, and asking for ours in return. There is no other choice than to come forward and closer, letting our skin rise to the same temperature of everything that surrounds us.

Opening our hearts and participating more fully in experiences might sound pretty on paper. It can conjure images of feel-good self-expression and anxiety-free joy. But in practice, it's a full-bodied affair that demands everything of us. It asks us to head directly into the fray, even in the face of our histories of hurt and preconceived assumptions about pain. When we look at traditional depictions of the Strength card, we often find a figure approaching a beastie with an open palm spread with snacks, dropping pretense and power flexes to courageously coax even the biggest jungle cat into fancy feast fluffiness.

STRENGTH

In Strength, we must commit to going first. And we must make that move with all of us, leaving nothing behind, holding nothing back, and with no assurance that we won't get burned. But this is not an exercise in poor boundaries or needless repeats of senseless pain. Instead, it's about exercising our right to love life through thick and thin—no longer playing hard to get, and taking our shot by showing our hand. It's about knowing that a lifetime of carefully guarded hurts is only going to hurt us, in the end. People are going to do us dirty sometimes. But sometimes, just sometimes, when we take a chance and open again, anyway, we find that others rise to meet our sweet sincerity.

Even the tiniest of love taps on the brick wall of a blocked situation can bring it tumbling down. One touch tells the other that we're human, too—with our own hopes and fears. Unarmed and available in our humanness, this action of unflexing inspires every creature around us to unclench its jaws and come just a hair closer. Just like small children and pets can often sense who and what to trust, when we become earnest with our intentions, all of existence gets coaxed by our candor.

We may think we need a secret weapon or a strategy to somehow "win" at life and best its battles. To secure our place on top by forcing another's hand forward, or by playing it close to the chest and holding it all in reserve. But whenever we work with this card, our warmth is all we ever need. And it never needs to be weaponized. When we **choose warm blood over cold comfort**, we choose to open up instead of closing ourselves off against new experiences. We also give ourselves over as a gift to this world: when we put ourselves out there, everyone gets to enjoy our glow. Strength tells us to stay open, stay with, and stay alive to the fact that every time we come heart-first, we remember that this one-and-only life is a love story, in the end.

 TURF TIP Explore Strength through landscapes that disarm and undress. Think petting zoos, sharing circles, saunas, and stuffed animal pile-ups.

ASK YOURSELF:

What am I arming myself against, and what am I seeking to protect?

Is this approach working, and at what cost?

How am I holding my history of heart hurts in my present-day life, and what no longer needs to be held close to the chest?

Where might I be waiting for someone else to share their feelings first, and why?

How can I step forward and show more of my hand? What does vulnerability look like for me?

THE SUN: The Real Deal

Stepping into this card's climate can feel slimmed down and straightforward, full of primary shapes. We ask ourselves, "Could that feeling I'm feeling really just be love?" "Is this quality that's expressing in this moment really a part of me?" "Can I believe what this person is showing me right now?" And in answering ourselves, it's easy to second-guess and hesitate. But when the Sun arrives, it's a chance to step directly into its light: clean, clear, and uncomplicated. The Sun tells us that what we are experiencing is self-evident. And that when we let our experiences, partnerships, and personhood reveal themselves, we **allow each thing to become more of what it already is**. In this sunlit land of acceptance, all of us can thrive in our own style.

There is a heart of hearts that sits in the center of each person and thing that already contains the essence that leads toward its next leap. This doesn't mean that some things are unalterably implanted with good or bad seeds. Rather, that each of us is a tiny acorn destined to become a full tree—already encoded with our greatness, and growing toward it courtesy of a micro master plan that naturally arises from our marrow. Whenever we work with this card, we're invited to consider the core meaning of where we find ourselves: forgoing the fancified "could be" explanations or one-day-might-be scenarios, and regarding whatever we know to be realest right now.

We can start to honor the fundamental feeling tones of the Sun's radiant realness by embracing the expressions that feel most authentic in a given moment: crying when it's our moment to cry, singing when it's our moment to sing, in whatever way we feel is right. And when we express this essence without analysis, we can start to respect the way others radiate, too. It's just you being you and them being them, says the Sun. This doesn't mean we abdicate responsibility for our own behavior, let others off the hook, or refuse to let life evolve. Instead, it means that we take responsibility for revealing whatever realness exists and responding as genuinely as we can, moving across life's light-up floor by the grace of our own ability to bear more bareness.

Ultimately, this card helps us find constancy by cutting through the elaborate layers and just living life as it is. Yes, there are all kinds of textured experiences that unfold in our lives with subtle arthouse nuance. But the Sun reminds us that there's also a beautifully basic, universally felt level on which it all splashes across the screen. Love stories. Sob stories. Adventure tales. There are only so many human dramas, and we've all got 'em. And when we embrace the core of whatever cinematic theme is showing up right now and inhabit its expression fully, we find that we're all living life on earth under the same sun.

TURF TIP Explore the Sun through landscapes that show themselves in their simple glory. Think birthday celebrations, morning coffee perches, nude beaches, and picnic spots.

ASK YOURSELF:

What's showing itself right now, and how am I showing up for it?

If I could reduce this life moment to just a few words or feelings, what would they be?

What's "realest" right now? What is the simplest solution or the least complicated approach?

How can I adopt a response that will feel most authentically me?

What basic human drama is unfolding right now and how could naming that basicness help me feel more beautifully human?

_____

_____

_____

_____

_____

_____

_____

_____

_____

_____

_____

_____

_____

_____

_____

_____

THE MINOR ARCANA

After exploring the big old biospheres of the Majors, you're ready to get nitty-gritty with the on-the-ground teachings of the Minors. Let the next few weeks of the month feel like a living laboratory as you practice responding to these cards by taking direct action and noticing how they show up in your everyday life.

The 5, 6, and 7 of Wands:
FEELING OURSELVES

As we show up to the solar-lit landscapes of Strength and the Sun, we can look to this trio of Minor Arcana kiddies to show up *for* ourselves—keeping the source of our inner glow good to go, no matter who's feeling it. You can think of this trio as *your endless summer*—using each card to commune with a beach blanket form of beingness that comfortably exposes its bare skin; keeps its honest and earnest temps steady; believes in the soap operatic pleasures of a paperback; and never needs an extra layer to keep life at bay.

THE 5 OF WANDS

This card is a shake-and-bake 5 that's fit for getting tossed in the spiciest flavors of self. We can show up in this 5's energy like tiny kids having a tantrum when the sunscreen comes out because they want to bound back onto the beach. But its orneriness actually wants to remind us that we can "have it out" with ourselves without losing heart. The 5 of Wands asks us to stick by our own sides through any

interior scuffles and forge a ride-or-die loyalty—bumping up against our own edges without fearing a breakup.

What am I railing against, and how can I let myself "have it out" right now; and how might this actually deepen my self-love?

_____
_____
_____
_____
_____
_____
_____
_____
_____

Tarot To-Do: Get physical in this energy, releasing yourself into a room like a baby animal who's been cooped up for the day. Bump up against the walls. Push off the furniture. Let out little yelps. Shake it down and out and off, noticing how these actions can have a surprisingly cleansing effect. When you're finally spent, fall into a pile— listening in for the clarity of your heartbeat, feeling the simplicity of your sweat, and reminding yourself that you're still here by your own side.

THE 6 OF WANDS

A 6 whose scent gets us high on our own life, this card invites us to embrace the supersized sensation of riding on top. This doesn't mean besting anything in battle, or securing gold-star evidence of excellence from the outside world. Instead, it's about letting larger-than-life-ness into our lives and beholding our own beautiful bigness. It asks us to take pleasure in the epic quality of our existence, no matter the scale of our achievements, and to give ourselves the gift of some good drama. Whatever your life is made of, you are the one who has made it, and this 6 wants you to pen your name to the story in neon lights.

How can I elevate some element of my everyday existence to larger-than-life status?
Where might I be playing down something that wants to be emphasized?

_____

_____

_____

_____

_____

_____

_____

_____

_____

Tarot To-Do: Imagine that your life was being made into a movie or bestselling beach read. What title would you choose? What events would be showcased? You might even design the cover or movie poster, and plan out the accompanying playlist. Notice how this gesture of aggrandizing your existence can remind you of your innate dignity.

THE 7 OF WANDS

Each tarot 7 asks us to graduate from a comfy level of existence where we might not be challenging ourselves sufficiently. In the fiery Wands, the invitation is about stepping up to claim our right to be recognized as special. Each one of us has "our thing"—some precious part of us that is the only one of its kind. And when this card comes calling, we might feel like we've lost touch with it, or have to scramble to trademark it before it gets plagiarized or runs out. But whatever our "thing," this distinctive essence is irreplaceable and inexhaustible, and the 7 of Wands reminds us that there's no one else who can do it quite like we do.

What is one bit of my inner beauty that no one else could ever duplicate?

_____

_____

_____

_____

_____

_____

_____

_____

Tarot To-Do: Imagine that someone was going to attend a costume party dressed as you. First, explore the go-to garb that would be able to easily pass as part of your personhood. But then, take a look at the gestures and energetic expressions that would be much harder to replicate. What do these original aspects reveal about the parts of you that don't have to be guarded to keep on glowing?

THE COURT CARDS

Having acclimatized to the Majors' themes and lived out the Minors' on-the-ground energies, you're now ready to try the Court Cards on for size. Let the final few weeks of the month inspire an identity exploration: using the four "styles" sketched below to see how you're channeling this card's archetype, and/or adding your own way of embodying it to the list.

The King of Wands: SHARE YOUR GIFTS

Each of the Kings is here to hold the room: exercising the magnetic power of their own presence with ease. In the Wands, we're asked to embrace our basic right to feel ourselves, and feel ourselves being felt. This King wants to open us to a mutual warmth where we joyfully give out the sparkles the world most needs right now, and our gifts are received with equal joy.

We can look to this King whenever we feel disconnected from our natural talents. If we're shy about stepping out to share them, or unsure that our light can contribute to the collective glow, it reassures us that what we're available to share in this moment is exactly the right thing to give.

Tap this King to step into a self-designed style of offering more of yourself to the world. Join life's gift exchange by sampling the presents below to see which you're packing.

What gift do you already have to give?

_____

_____

_____

_____

_____

_____

_____

_____

_____

KING OF WANDS

THE GRACIOUS HOST. This style of sharing showcases your gift of welcoming others into the width of your warmth. Maybe you're the type who inspires the people and energies around you to relax and unwind through judgment-free expansiveness. Allow all of life to find a home around you as you settle into yourself.

THE CAKE TOPPER. This style of sharing showcases your extra-special touch. Maybe you're a "closer"—here to contribute that finishing flair to a life moment that brings it all together. Let yourself swoop in and leave little cherries behind, depositing a contribution—however mini—that says "I was here."

THE PARTY PLATTER. This style of sharing showcases the diversity of your gifts and responsiveness to the needs of the moment. Maybe you feel like you're a little bit good at many things but never truly great. Instead of self-criticizing, choose to revel in the range of toothpick tasties you have to offer as you see what needs serving up.

THE FLOWER ARRANGEMENT. This style of sharing showcases your ability to draw out natural beauty and vivify the rooms you enter. Maybe you're the type who contributes by noticing what's gorgeous and throwing it into relief through enhancement and appreciation. Trust that when you just feel good, plain and simple, the world glows brighter.

The Signature Scent Spread

....

August's energy gifts us a personalized perfume that no one else has. Sniffing into our own specialness can sometimes feel like a struggle, as we start to compare and contrast our flair with all the finery that surrounds us. And sometimes our own fragrance is elusive: there are moments in which we simply can't seem to catch a whiff of what is wholly ours. Use the spread below to explore the truest elements of your essence so you can share your scent with the world.

If you pull cards that you see as confronting in some way, or as "negative" qualities to possess, take a moment to pause and consider the elements of their meaning. These qualities might actually be part of your secret superpower! For example: if you pull the 9 of Swords—which is associated with facing what frightens us—maybe one of your sweetest strengths is the ability to help unmask the scaries inside yourself and others.

*Card 1: **The Base Note.*** This card represents the foundational part of your self-expression. Explore which of its qualities can help stabilize your sense of you-ness. You can use this energy to give you solid ground when you feel like you've lost track of who you really are.

*Card 2: **The Middle Note.*** This card is your "heart note"—the part of your personal perfume that is meant to be savored solo. Explore which of its qualities you can give more of to yourself privately. You can use this energy to connect with your internal resplendence.

*Card 3: **The Top Note.*** Your shareable essence, this card represents the part of you that's meant to be spread around without reservation. Explore which of its qualities you can express more fully in the world. Trust that you have enough of its goodness within you to go around.

MAGIC TRICK:
A Grand Romance

August is all about kicking up the brightness on our born-to-bedazzle glow. Turn the same-old stuff in your life into larger-than by using your cards as experiential enhancements. When you pull one, consider how you might turn it "up." How can you let the fullest form of its meaning play out in your life? This doesn't mean faking feelings you don't feel, or creating needless drama out of nothing. Instead, let each card feel like a Valentine and answer its call with your whole heart. If you catch a tiny inkling of that card's meaning in your life right now, give it your full attention and watch it grow. Or consciously court a card, selecting one from your deck and giving it a day in the sun. Treat it like a lover you'd love to learn everything about. Don't hold back from your deck and it won't hold back from you.

August Tarotscopes

LEO: *The 6 of Wands.* Your love for larger-than-lifeness sometimes gets a rep for melodrama, but it's actually evidence of your ability to add extra-special sparkle to the everyday. Take August to be extra "extra," unapologetic in your love for the ginormous.

VIRGO: *Strength.* A hands-on healer here to draw out the finest in your fellow humans, August is your invite to embrace your status as a cheerleader by leading with love. Let your own heart-baring moments inspire the rest of the world to trust, too.

LIBRA: *The King of Wands.* A reflector and reverberator, you know how to read the world's response to your every move. Take August to let this reflection be an opportunity to relish your resplendence rather than refine your approach. Lap up only the feedback that feels finest.

SCORPIO: *The 6 of Wands.* You're an intense friend who knows the stakes of this existence, and August is your invite to be exhilarated by this epicness. Courageously charge up with whatever pulls feel most powerful within you, relishing your role as the star of the show.

SAGITTARIUS: *The Sun.* Forever on the hunt for extra clues, you love to read life's hidden messages and interpret the esoterica. Let August remind you that even the simplest forms of existence can also be fascinating, digging into the very real mysteries of what's actually here.

CAPRICORN: *Strength.* Your power is packed in like hard earth, here for you to have and hold for life. Let August's energies help you soften your grasp ever so slightly, reminding you that vital force can also be found by showing your hand—unarmed, unclenched, and unflexed.

AQUARIUS: *The King of Wands.* A cool-handed operator who conjures whole worlds in the blink of an eye, August is your chance to celebrate your imprint on creation. Lap up some of the long-distance light you've been giving out and claim authorship of your place in the sun.

PISCES: *The Sun.* A psychic sponge that sucks up invisible intel, you're forever feeling beyond what can be seen. Take August to commune with the energies you can actually glimpse with the naked eye, diving into direct conversations and relishing the clarity that comes in the light of day.

ARIES: *The 5 of Wands.* The zodiac's most scintillating spark, you love to instigate. Let August be your month to actually celebrate this push-and-pull power. Bring curiosity and consciousness toward combative moments, and let outbursts feel cleansing and cathartic.

TAURUS: *The 7 of Wands.* If left to your own devices, your tendency to acquire can sometimes verge on hoarding. You seek to lock it all down for life. Let August remind you that your internal treasures will never be taken *from* you, because no one can ever take the precious place *of* you.

GEMINI: *The 7 of Wands.* Moved by the world's many wonders, you glean inspiration from life's bazaar. August is here to remind you that this mixtape approach to existence doesn't make your creations any less "yours." Trust that whatever you touch bears the mark of your inimitable style.

CANCER: *The 5 of Wands.* In the name of keeping your beloveds close, you sometimes close yourself off from conflict. Let August be an opportunity to express even your most difficult emotions without fearing that you'll lose love. The keepers will still be there after the storm.

As you depart August's full-hearted honeymoon for September's carefully cultivated vineyards, start to sort through all of the precious parts of your life. Notice the divine detail of your physical environment and daily rituals, and identify the magical role that each imperfectly perfect piece contributes to the whole.

Now, gather your August and September cards into two separate piles and pluck a pal from each pack. August's cutie represents what wants to be left to its own, naturally expressed devices. September's selection reps what wants to be nurtured, attended to, and further refined.

Bow down at the altar of your deck. Dedicate yourself to the witchy woods that wile within you and it. In September's delicate ecosystem, knowing our own nature lets us take our place within nature itself . . .

This month's tarot cards beckon us to bend without ever breaking: *How will you work your magic?*

SEPTEMBER

The Magic of Devotion

In the Stars: September is alchemized through the Mutable Earth energy of Virgo. Mutable energy responds, and Earth energy ritualizes. In January and May, we met Earth through Capricorn's gravity and Taurus' richness. This month, we're ready for a final fling with the element through Virgo's Mercury-ruled experience, which metabolizes earthly matter and sieves what's most valuable to the surface. A tangible way to access Virgo energy is by honoring the natural order of things: the sacred geometry of honeybees' hexagonal cells; the symphony of changing seasons; your body's processes. All of nature finds its place instinctually by answering to its own calls, and you are a part of this—here to contribute the particular magic of your makeup to the holy wild whole.

In the Cards: September's cardstock is a carefully coiled cauldron, and each of its six archetypes is an invite to explore our integrity—the quality of being whole unto ourselves as we meet the world. These cards demand our devotion, a notion that might conjure images of submissive genuflection. But when applied consciously, devotion is about cultivating a supple responsiveness to life that also respects our own intactness: we learn our limits and revere our gifts so we're ready to respond to what arises, as we are, with what we've got. They are the deck's promise rings. Use them to wed yourself to who you are and what merits your magic; and know that you can always give yourself to these cards on your own terms.

In Your Life: To apprentice yourself to September's art of allegiance, you can embrace a **daily practice** of "everyday divinity": venerating the sacredness of your life by attending to its details; discerning what wants to be "worked on" and drawing more of its value out through gradual change and care-filled cultivation; employing rituals that best support your sensitivities; and enjoying some sweet solitude so you can better learn about the witchy wonders that make up the whole of you. In a world that often aggrandizes the obvious and denies subtlety, September asks us to pay attention to every particle: mining more magic from even the tiniest bits.

ZODIAC SIGN: Virgo
ELEMENT: Earth
QUALITY: Mutable
CARDS: the Hermit; the Magician; the 8/9/10 of Pentacles; the Knight of Pentacles
MAGIC WORDS: Integrity. Craft. Alchemy. Discernment. Witchery.

⇒ MONTH'S DEBUT ⇐
MAJOR ARCANA

Take the first few weeks of the month to land in these card landscapes—orienting yourself to their themes and exploring their turf through meditation and visualization. You may also want to return to the inquiry questions as part of your daily practice.

The Hermit + The Magician

September's pair of Major Arcana deities are our *self-study sieves*: here to help us sort through our energetic contents, understand our constitutions, and apply our resources where they're needed most. An exercise in observation and filtration, when we pull these cards, or choose to work with them intentionally, it's an opportunity to sensitively survey the intricacies that make up our interior. Once we've processed our particularities, we can start to pan for more gold: noticing how each precious part of us can better serve the world's sacred geometry.

THE HERMIT: Table for One

This card is a solitary walkabout through a forest where no one else but us witnesses the weather. Its climate is entirely self-sustaining. Maybe it's an alfresco table for one at the edge of a lapis lazuli ocean, where we sip from a salt-rimmed cup whose nectar is utterly unrepresentable to others in our vacation photos. Or it's a backroom booth covered in red leather where we pour from a carafe, leaning in to listen to the secrets that can only be shared between self and self. However we choose to dine, the Hermit serves up a dish best enjoyed solo, asking **who we really are when we are wholly alone**.

Bearing witness to our contents, unaccompanied and unadorned, is an enormous act of courage that yields priceless private pleasures. Whenever this card comes a-calling, we're asked to renew our lease on a room that's entirely ours. This doesn't mean we have to leave our lovers and friends for a literal hermitage, cutting off connection or crawling into a cave without a trace. Instead, in its earthy, Virgo-ruled energy, we're asked to keep on inhabiting life while also taking up residence in this most private of places: being in the world while also being unto ourselves.

IX

THE HERMIT

Like a casita contained on a family property, or a weekend-for-one that we book on the fly with every intention of returning on Monday, the Hermit wants us to rendezvous with self without having to abandon anything else.

This archetype is our exercise in daily divinity, an extension of the inner sanctum we found when we embodied the High Priestess. While we listened deeply in the High Priestess, we're now asked to watch and learn: apprenticing ourselves to our changing processes by being completely "with" the person we are right now. Imagine a movie where a mature divorcé books a trip to Tuscany, slowly coming alive again in their own style and time, as they learn to roll fresh pasta and saunter across the rolling hills. Wherever we choose to travel, the Hermit invites us to let our retreats return us to ourselves, as we are in this very moment. From this place of integration, we can venerate the wisdom from our time walking the earth thus far and can continue on our path.

Many representations of this archetype illuminate a figure whose lantern only lights up each particular step as it goes, and entering this card asks us to trust our personalized process and walk alongside ourselves arm in arm, at whatever our pace. Virgo rules this card, and this astrological sign is commonly associated with the symbol of "the virgin." Stripped of its complicated lineage and associations, the virgin is an unwed being who lives only by their own code—divining who and what to open toward with complete discernment and internal wholeness. When the Hermit comes into our lives, we're asked to bow at this altar of self, renewing our lifelong vows with whatever world awaits within. The Hermit shows us that when we commit to being truly *with* the person we are right now—in all our particularity—we can be on, and by, our own side, through thick and thin.

 TURF TIP Explore the Hermit through landscapes that are devoted to their own codes. Think places of personal pilgrimage, self-guided tours, choose-your-own-toppings bars, and tables for one.

ASK YOURSELF:

What is my relationship to solitude? How do I define the difference between being alone and loneliness?

Who am I when I'm solo with myself, and how does that person compare to the being who shows up in company?

What would it look like to inhabit a room of my own, and how would I design this space?

How do I honor my own rites of passage?

What wants to be ritualized in my life right now?

What vows with myself need to be renewed?

_____

_____

_____

_____

_____

_____

_____

_____

_____

_____

_____

_____

_____

_____

THE MAGICIAN (PART DEUX): Metabolizing Magic

THE MAGICIAN

In June's Gemini-ruled energy, we meet this card in its expressions of interception and inspiration, exploring how we open up to life's possibilities and welcome what wants to come through our channel. The planet Mercury—which governs both Gemini and Virgo—marks the Magician card, but returns here in September in a slightly different flavor.

In this earthier form, this card shifts us from the airy inhale-exhale of the breath into the body's metabolic rate. Like wondrous weather vanes who both tune in to the current conditions and attune our systems to it, this expression of the Magician asks us how we're assimilating our life experiences, and how we can better serve the sensitivities of our spirit's nervous system. A more adaptable, mobile form of the Hierophant's floor-to-ceiling storehouse of embodied belief, when we work with the Magician in this way, we can start to inquire about how experiences actually affect us. How do we process the power and impact of each and every life moment? How do we decide which bits get fully digested and released, and which become more permanent parts of our bones? When we understand how we process life, our sensitivities can become an integral part of our creative process—as we learn to make use of the matter that moves through us in our own way.

 TURF TIP Explore this form of the Magician through landscapes that are highly attuned to their intricate processes. Think ant farms, vineyards, weather stations, and cooking classes.

ASK YOURSELF:

What is my metaphorical metabolic rate right now?

Do I need a lot of time to assimilate a current experience, or am I grab-and-go carb-loading and burning it all off at breakneck speed?

How do I get affected by life—am I someone who takes up and takes on a lot from my environment, or does life seem to slide off my back?

How can I creatively utilize what's moving through me?

_____

_____

_____

_____

_____

_____

_____

_____

_____

_____

_____

_____

_____

_____

_____

_____

_____

_____

Your Planetary Planner

September asks us to connect with the divine on the daily. When you're feeling overwhelmed by to-do lists and calendar invites, you can use the list below to come into a different kind of cosmic rhythm that takes its cues from the ancient planetary rulers. You might also explore that day's ruling tarot card, flipping to its monthly inquiry questions for more guidance. And for a special touch, find out what day of the week you were born, and treat that day's planet and card as your personal guides.

Monday *(The Moon: The High Priestess):* Invites us to listen deeply, giving ourselves more space and silence to receive messages from our inner font. Take a moment to welcome emptiness before you rush to fill up.

Tuesday *(Mars: The Tower):* Invites us to relish the life force that courses through us and everything around us. Have a little fun with friction, whether it's a sweaty run, or coming clean through a direct confrontation.

Wednesday *(Mercury: The Magician):* Invites us to attune to subtle signs from our environment. Explore the creative channel that is you—seeing where you might adapt your approach, and soothing your nervous system as needed.

Thursday *(Jupiter: The Wheel of Fortune):* Invites us to exhale into something bigger and find faith in the adventure. Risk going beyond your usual comfy zone and press pause on over-planning.

Friday *(Venus: The Empress):* Invites us to become available for more—amplifying our capacity to receive life's delights. Stay present for pleasure, and take in experiences without having to put out.

Saturday *(Saturn: The World):* Invites us to consider our gravitas and establish limits. Tap sources of security that strengthen you, and lay down firm boundaries that honor what matters most.

Sunday *(The Sun: The Sun):* Invites us to connect with our core self and embrace simplicity. Play with expressing your emotions vividly, and generously sharing more of your essence with the wide world.

THE MINOR ARCANA

After exploring the big old biospheres of the Majors, you're ready to get nitty-gritty with the on-the-ground teachings of the Minors. Let the next few weeks of the month feel like a living laboratory, as you practice responding to these cards by taking direct action, and noticing how they show up in your everyday life.

The 8, 9, and 10 of Pentacles:
PERSONAL ALCHEMY

As we use the Hermit and the Magician to sort and sift through the matter of which we are made, we can look to this triplet of Minor Arcana kiddies to engage in some personal alchemy: honestly assessing our natural gifts, and refining our expertise without trying to fix our flaws. You can think of this triplet as *your vineyard*. Each card is a chance to peruse the particular territory that makes up you, and to get the best juice out of your life's grapes by both nourishing your nature and responding to the current weather conditions.

THE 8 OF PENTACLES

In this particular swirl of the infinity-looping 8s, we open up our wet clay to getting worked on at the potter's wheel of life. Always in apprenticeship to some process, this card asks us to practice submitting to being shaped—giving in without giving up any of our integrity. When we release the power play of having to control the push and pull, we render ourselves pliable enough to learn more about our own matter as it's molded.

What is my process right now—and how can I let myself be in process?

_____
_____
_____
_____
_____
_____
_____
_____
_____
_____

Tarot To-Do: Look around the world and notice how almost everything is always in an alchemical state of becoming, and identify the in-between states you see. The hideaway oven habitat where the casserole gets cooking. The nearly imperceptible growth starting to spill from the window box. Your kiddo's latest attempt at a piano tune. Sketch out some of the visible and invisible processes that are contributing to these efforts, recognizing that nothing ever really needs to reach some heightened state of total realization to be valuable.

THE 9 OF PENTACLES

Perhaps the most private of all the 9s' treehouse pockets, in the Pentacles suit we're asked to fold into the sensuality of solitude. In this card, we use all of the knowledge about our intricacies to treat ourselves even better, becoming our own personal assistants who serve ourselves straight from a self-styled platter. Its energy asks us to know our nature so well that we can nurture ourselves with what suits it: hand-selecting the jewels that best bring out the color in our own eyes and sitting down at our own table to enjoy the fruits we've farmed to it.

How do I define my personal palate? What are my tastes and what do these reveal about who I am? What would it look like to treat myself well in this moment?

_____

_____

_____

_____

_____

_____

_____

_____

_____

Tarot To-Do: Imagine that you were a treasured guest being invited into your own home, and explore what you'd want to provide for yourself to make your stay complete. What would your environmental needs be: the colors, scents, sounds, and flavors that would help you feel most at home in the holiness of you? You might even picture what you envisioned about adulthood as a kid: listening in to the luxuries of self-directed solitude you imagined that you'd have the opportunity to enjoy when you finally "grew up," and serving them to yourself now.

THE 10 OF PENTACLES

The 10s always offer up the full shebang of their suit's elemental energy, and in the earthy Pentacles we're invited to explore what it means to "have it all." We can sometimes struggle with the sense that our lives remain incomplete—wondering if someday we'll finally "make it." In service of soothing this struggle, this card asks us to have more of what we've already got and acknowledge the value in each imperfectly perfect piece of our present lives. When we give up the impossible quest to have it all, we can find wholeness by making the very most out of everything that's gathered at our feet.

What do I believe that I'm missing, and how can I make more out of what's already here?

_____

_____

_____

_____

_____

_____

_____

_____

_____

Tarot To-Do: Imagine what a complete portrait of your life would look like. Explore the people, places, and things you'd want to pack into the frame to form a comprehensive picture of your life. Notice which of these elements might be memories of the past, or mirages representing the future: has-beens and not-yet-to-bes. For the elements in your portrait that no longer exist, or don't exist yet, explore what person, place, or thing you might summon from your life right now that would help you feel its presence.

THE COURT CARDS

Having acclimatized to the Majors' themes and lived out the Minors' on-the-ground energies, you're now ready to try the Court Cards on for size. Let the final few weeks of the month inspire an identity exploration: using the four "styles" sketched below to see how you're channeling this card's archetype, and/or adding your own way of embodying it to the list.

The Knight of Pentacles: LISTEN TO YOUR BODY

Each Knight is a magic medium here to help us let energies pass through us and shift our approach to meet the moment. Here, in September's Virgo-ruled Earth turf, we respond to life through our physicality. With this Knight's help, we can better support our nervous systems by divining our proper pacing and availability to take on what's unfolding around us. By working with our body's natural intelligence, we learn how to "take the shape" of what's arriving in our lives: letting it change us without permanently altering our form.

So often we find ourselves contorting against life, believing that we've got to brace our bodies against big feelings to remain in control. But the tighter we grip against, the more likely we are to snap, and this Knight asks us to get more supple in our approach. Instead of charging at confronting life situations, we can learn to dance.

Tap this Knight by listening in to how your body wants to respond to life right now. Select one of the styles below to help your form become more fit to face whatever's arising.

How can you best serve your own shape?

_____

_____

_____

_____

_____

_____

KNIGHT OF PENTACLES

BODY HEAT: Maybe you find yourself in a life moment that's asking for some compression and consistent touch. This could be a situation where you feel untethered, as emotions pull you in multiple directions. Support your body by first giving yourself some anchors. Practices might include a weighted blanket, hot stones, or packing yourself in sand.

THE CELESTIAL BODY: Maybe you find yourself in a life moment that's asking for a very light, almost imperceptible touch. This could be a situation that's confronting you head-on and just seems like "too much" to handle. Support your body by letting yourself pan out and disconnect. Practices might include remote reiki, a sensory deprivation tank, or simply checking out by staring into space.

BODY + SOUL: Maybe you find yourself in a life moment that's asking for you to really "get in there" and work it out. This could be a situation that feels like it's been stuck for too long, or one that dredges up buried stories and emotions. Support your body by engaging in some vigorous movement. Practices might include a super-sweaty run, deep tissue massage, or all-out dance party.

THE BODY SCAN: Maybe you find yourself in a life moment that's asking for an intuitive, adaptive approach. Support your body by observing its subtlest signs and responding in kind. Practices might include an actual body scan, targeted aromatherapy, or a slow hike.

The Multivitamin Spread

....

September's energies are a proprietary blend of personalized power and real-time responsiveness—inviting us to calibrate our inner contents so we can move through the outer world in integrity. Use this spread below to explore what card archetypes want to do their work on you right now and how you can work with them to serve the whole you.

You can "treat yourself" by choosing just one of the cards or a combo and applying them to a particular life situation like a power poultice. Maybe you're struggling to move on after a big change, and need a "bone-builder" and "blood-builder" card mix to restore stability and inspire passion; or you're trying to make sense of a confusing experience and could use the "probiotic" card to help you process. As you pull each card, also notice when an archetype feels like it's here to do something *to* you, and feel into how you might allow it to do something *through* you instead. Trust that you can send each card's nutrients to the parts of your life where they're most needed.

Card 1: **The Bone-builder.** This card represents a durable energy that wants to render you more calcium-rich. Let its meaning help give you shape and structure. Unequivocally turn toward it and allow this face-to-face to offer your spirit some spinach.

Card 2: **The Blood-builder.** This card represents a vitalizing energy that wants to bring you closer to the heart of your life-force. Allow its meaning to increase the natural flow of your passionate purpose. Let your reaction to it invigorate your system and inspire bold moves.

Card 3: **The Probiotic.** This card represents a cooperative energy that wants to restore balance and help you digest experience. Let its meaning move you toward subtle intuitive hits about where things might feel "off" and how you can process your life right now.

Card 4: **The Antioxidant.** This card represents a protective energy that wants to safe-guard your sensitive system against life's assaults. Let leaning toward its meaning ease areas of overextended stress, and free up your energies in service of greater nourishment.

MAGIC TRICK:
Hone Your Craft

September asks us to divine our singular style of magic and devote ourselves in service to it. Take this time to explore what kind of tarot reader you are and how you'd like to ritualize your practice. Begin by taking an inventory of what you think a tarot reader "should" be like, and how you think you may or may not align with this image. Then, start to notice the kind of practice that would actually fit who you are and the skills you have to share. Maybe you're a no-nonsense kitchen witch whose wisdom is as strong and straightforward as black coffee. This kind of witchery might be best served by daily pulls that focus on direct "to-dos," keeping your cards out on the table like Post-its. Maybe you're a full-bodied being who has to live the cards completely, in which case you might massage the meaning out of a single card over the course of weeks or a month and erect a large-scale altar to it. Or maybe you're a dream queen who reads symbols more loosely and abstractly, and want to bob in and out of your practice and stay open to many meanings. Whatever your style, honor your witchery and take September to further hone it.

September Tarotscopes

VIRGO: *The 9 of Pentacles.* You're so steeped in self-knowledge that you're forever aware of what could be adjusted, just so. September asks you to nourish this wisdom about your own nature. Let knowing the particulars of your palate help you serve up what's most pleasurable.

LIBRA: *The Hermit.* You're a being who loves to learn more about yourself through dialogue with others. But this month, you're asked to uncover the magic in some monologuing. Find solace in solitary moments and enjoy a rendezvous with the mystery that is you.

SCORPIO: *The Magician.* You can bear the beasts in life like the best of them, enduring the raw range of human emotion. But September wants you to acknowledge the sensitivities of your system, too. Take time to process the power of your emo experiences so you can integrate them into your battle-hardened whole.

SAGITTARIUS: *The Knight of Pentacles.* A mover and shaker who loves slipping into whatever the local color, September is your invite to explore these shape-shifts on a physical level. Notice how you can soften your body to let more of life in instead of bracing for impact.

CAPRICORN: *The 9 of Pentacles.* The finest wine in the zodiac's cellar, you understand the benefits and wisdoms of maturity. Let September be an opportunity to order up the good stuff that fits your well-honed specifications. Demand the highest quality on offer and lap it up luxuriously.

AQUARIUS: *The 8 of Pentacles.* Blessed with the ability to summarize the take-home points in an instant, you sometimes forget that you don't have to know

it all. Let September be a lesson in embracing the process, apprentice-style. You're allowed to be human just like the rest of us.

 PISCES: *The 10 of Pentacles.* Here to hold life in its entirety, there's nothing that escapes your empathetic embrace. Let September remind you that you truly have it all without having to feel swamped. Swap feelings of overwhelm for veneration of the vast array of emotions at your disposal.

 **ARIES:** *The 8 of Pentacles.* You're on this earth to crack the shell without worrying about the consequences. September wants you to embrace this ability to apply your eager efforts to whatever crosses your path. Give it a go with whatever you've got and don't worry about how good you are at it.

 **TAURUS:** *The Magician.* You know how to glean nourishment from life's nibbles and can easily absorb the riches from any situation. Take September to refine this process of powering up by exercising your right to discern. Savor the situations that fortify you, and leave the rest on the table.

 **GEMINI:** *The Hermit.* You're a backpacked, be-sneakered kiddo who loves to curiously cross life's thresholds. Let September be a chance to mark your personal rites of passage and each step along your chosen path. Bear witness to your maturations and changes with wonder.

 CANCER: *The Knight of Pentacles.* Your superpowers activate when you take a compassionate, curvaceous shape. September reminds you that this ability to "take on" energy and respond doesn't have to feel powerless. Instead, explore how becoming a vessel can make you feel even more fit for life.

 LEO: *The 10 of Pentacles.* A grand finale furball, you often live like it's your last night on earth. September wants you to translate your ability to have it all into appreciation for all that you already have. This month, devote your attention to adoring each part of your life that's here.

*A*s you leave September's tended vineyard and head for October's curated gallery, regard the contours of your world and how things fit together. Maybe it's the seamless slide of a key card in a hotel room slot. Or the ideal sugar-to-cream ratio in your coffee cup. Explore what clicks into place perfectly, and what appears to be out of place and in need of retrofitting.

Now, gather your September and October cards into two separate piles and pluck a pal from each pack. Let September's pick represent a non-negotiable part of your inner code. And use October's archetype to begin making moves in alignment with this commitment.

Take a good look into your deck's magic mirror. Stare straight into the eyes of each archetype without blinking. In October's daring daybreak, everything can find exactly the right light . . .

This month's tarot cards stand to face their own reflection: *What's near? What's far? And what's meeting you exactly where you are?*

OCTOBER

The Magic of Light

In the Stars: October is elevated by the Cardinal Air energy of Libra. Cardinal energy inspires, and Air energy enlightens. In February and June we met Air through the breadth of Aquarius and the breathability of Gemini. This month, Libran air becomes more rarefied, curated by the high standards of its ruling planet, Venus. A tangible way to access Libra energy is to watch things find their light: a morning stripe across your desk that beckons you to begin; the perfect proportions of a painting hung with care for its creator's intent. In October's synergistic sheen, we're asked to look upon our lives: examining everything that we think we are and are not, and have and haven't accomplished so far. At the clear-sighted crossroads, we gain the grace to aspire toward greatness by starting where we stand.

In the Cards: October's cardstock is made from symmetrical lines and clear parameters, and each of its seven archetypes is a chance to regard the scene before us and find our right fit within it. While the ideas of alignment and clarity might call to mind serene brushstrokes and everlasting peace, these cards remind us that finding like-a-glove jumpsuits and reaching enchanted high ground starts with standing up for what's right for us, right now. They are the deck's 20/20 vision. Let them throw your life into relief: courageously showing you exactly what's able to meet your gaze; giving you the strength to leave the rest in your peripherals; and keeping your eyes only on the prizes that are most perfect for you.

In Your Life: To see October's reflection most clearly, you can embrace a **daily practice** of "designing your life": exploring your standards and ideals, and the motivations behind them; noticing the process of cause and effect in your life—what you choose to champion, how your actions create reverb, and how you respond to others' output; and relishing your holiest hopes without losing sight of what's already here. A potent realignment for the entirety of our lives, October's magic can click into place only when we're willing to wield the sword and make the cuts.

ZODIAC SIGN: Libra
ELEMENT: Air
QUALITY: Cardinal
CARDS: Justice; the Empress; the Ace/2/3/4 of Swords; the Queen of Swords
MAGIC WORDS: Reflection. Alignment. Elevation. Clarity. Cause and Effect.

MAJOR ARCANA

Take the first few weeks of the month to land in these card landscapes—orienting yourself to their themes and exploring their turf through meditation and visualization. You may also want to return to the inquiry questions as part of your daily practice.

Justice + The Empress

October's pair of Major Arcana deities represents *the cosmos' fitting room*. They are a call to honestly assess the elements of our lives that can and cannot be altered, and to enhance the natural beauty of what best fits our forms. When we pull these cards, or choose to work with them intentionally, it's a chance to explore our sense of alignment. Where might we have gone astray from our center lines? How can we equilibrate our lives accordingly? How do our inner values match up with our outer worlds? We can use these cards to explore what feels viscerally right and wrong in our bodies and spirits, and to champion the causes that are best suited to our contours.

JUSTICE: Haute Couture

When we step into this card's climate, dawn streaks into the dressing room, and the fabric of our lives is illuminated in full color. We've had a solid night's sleep and we arrive in this walk-in closet with our prescription glasses on, and a cup of black coffee in our hands. Eyes open. Spine straight. Ready to celebrate what we've been wearing like a second skin, but also primed to purge the threads that are no longer a fit. With a clear line of sight, we summon the courage to reach for whatever feels most right, right now.

Whenever we work with this card, we're being asked to consider the fit of some element of our lives. It's a chance to divine our own, customized sense of right and wrong that goes far beyond any externally imposed rubrics of justness. Each of us is possessed of some internal rudder, which can change as we change—course-correcting over the course of our lives—but which nonetheless provides us with a way forward at any given moment. When Justice arrives,

JUSTICE

we're being asked to honestly assess the choices that have led us to the point where we now stand; and the choices we now have that could create different effects.

Maybe we're in a partnership that our friends keep telling us is not giving us "enough," but we're not ready to quit it—aware of secret bits of its worthiness, or still just living and learning on our own timeline. Maybe people we admire want to encourage us toward a professional development that seems like the logical next step but just feels dead wrong, despite the pros-and-cons list on paper. An exercise in existential equilibration, Justice wants to lead us toward the light that is ours alone, revealing that what is right for us may or may not appear rational to other people, and that **we have every right to answer to our own reasons**.

Just like a haute couture private fitting, the way that each of us senses right and wrong in our system will be completely bespoke. Some of us know instantly when something feels scratchy, tugging the fabric from our bodies before we're even zipped in. Others of us have to spend a while in the material—living and learning by partying till the break of dawn in dresses gone wrong. No matter our style of assessing and correcting, Justice reminds us that we can reckon with rightness without any indictments. Even the choices we end up making that feel "wrong" lead us closer toward our own version of right. You'll be done when you're done, says Justice. And you'll be ready when you're ready to wake up to a new morning's light. An illumination instead of an incriminating punishment for wrongdoings, Justice wants us to let the art of equilibration become an exaltation.

 TURF TIP Explore Justice through landscapes that are clearly contoured and unwavering in their equilibrium. Think the lines where earth meets sky, site-specific architecture, sculpture wings, and private fitting rooms.

ASK YOURSELF:

What are my personal definitions of right and wrong?

How do I respond when something within me or around me seems to deviate from the correct course?

What are the shoulds and the wants in my life, and how do these two realms sync up?

How do I back my internal sense of what's right when it may be at odds with the world around me?

Where do I feel "off," and what could help restore me to center?

What feels most right for me, right now?

_____

_____

_____

_____

_____

_____

_____

_____

_____

_____

_____

_____

_____

_____

THE EMPRESS (PART DEUX): Beauty Boosters

In May's earthy, Taurus-ruled energy, we met this card through the lens of more-ness: a buffet of lush abundance that asked us how much of the good stuff we could handle. And in October, with the planet Venus beckoning both Taurus and Libra into its boudoir, we get a chance to commune with this card once again, opening ourselves to its new, Air-ruled form of expression.

In October's energy, the Empress asks us to take our natural appetite for life and use it to elevate our menu. This month, the Empress tells us that we don't have to accept sub-par snacks. Instead, we're being invited to evaluate our own notion of value and use this to improve the quality of our lives. But the Empress isn't a rigid ruler who refuses to acknowledge humanness—this act of elevation offers us the chance to enhance our lives by defining our own beauty standards. Rather than just swallowing down what the world deems "good," we're asked to look at what surrounds us through our own eyes and decide what we want more of according to our personal tastes, needs, and value systems. Neither good vibes only nor all doom and gloom, this card beckons us to notice the natural bits of beauty that are present in our lives and to help them catch the light—encouraging ourselves and others to become the best of what we already are.

 TURF TIP Explore this form of the Empress through landscapes that easefully elevate and enhance. Think greenery after a flood of rain, mood lighting, pedestals and platforms, and room diffusers.

ASK YOURSELF:

Where am I on the negative-positive thinking spectrum and how can I find a balance between these poles?

What is my "best light"? What situations, contexts, and relationships naturally bring out and enhance the parts of myself that I like the most?

How do I support these acts of elevation and enhancement in others?

How do I craft my standards, and how do I uphold them?

What do I value most, and what does this reveal about my own worthiness?

_____

_____

_____

_____

_____

_____

_____

_____

_____

_____

_____

_____

_____

_____

_____

_____

_____

_____

Polarity Points

October asks us to see things from our other side and clarify our values through contrast. In astrology, the twelve zodiac signs are arranged into six pairs, or polarities, and each duet works with a similar theme from different points of view. You can use them to explore your own life cycles—looking at how themes that emerged in one month might find completion within the other.

Aries (April) + Libra (October): *The Axis of Confrontation.* Aries energy instigates and Libra considers the impact. Use this pair of months to balance the need for immediate action with the call to refine your aspirations.

Taurus (May) + Scorpio (November): *The Axis of Absorption.* Taurus energy fills us up and Scorpio empties the excess. Use this pair of months to balance the need to possess what you desire with the call to embrace natural cycles of change.

Gemini (June) + Sagittarius (December): *The Axis of Improvisation.* Gemini energy breathes life through, and Sag seeks signs of life everywhere. Use this pair of months to balance the need to meet the moment with the hunt for a higher meaning.

Cancer (July) + Capricorn (January): *The Axis of Protection.* Capricorn energy creates the container and Cancer shelters within it. Use this pair of months to balance the need for self-sufficient structures with the call to tend your own softness.

Leo (August) + Aquarius (February): *The Axis of Expression.* Leo energy steeps us in our special essence and Aquarius gives us the space to spread it around. Use this pair of months to balance the need to be seen with the call to become the seer.

Virgo (September) + Pisces (March): *The Axis of Veneration.* Virgo energy makes magic out of what's visible, and Pisces immerses us in the invisible. Use this pair of months to balance continued attention and cultivation with the call to come undone.

THE MINOR ARCANA

After exploring the big old biospheres of the Majors, you're ready to get nitty-gritty with the on-the-ground teachings of the Minors. Let the next few weeks of the month feel like a living laboratory as you practice responding to these cards by taking direct action and noticing how they show up in your everyday life.

The Ace, 2, 3, and 4 of Swords:
SETTING THE SCENE

As we let Justice and the Empress lead us into just the right light, we can look to October's quartet of Minor Arcana card kiddies to refine our vision by deciding what gets to take up space within it. You can think of this card crew as *your mise-en-scène*: just like a film director might arrange all the necessary elements in a given frame to convey the parts of the narrative that are most vital, each of these cards is a chance to adopt an empowered perspective. Use them to call the shots and crop the excess so you can hone in on exactly what wants to be seen.

THE ACE OF SWORDS

Each Ace is our goody bag of its element. It's a party pack that asks us to come alive to its fundamental charms and start wielding them in the world. In the airy Swords suit, we stand below the blank page of the sky at sunrise and are dazzled as the light of day starts to dance across life's surfaces. We can treat this slim Ace energy like a magic wand: tapping the tops of situations and relationships by asking questions and taking actions, and then courageously abiding the revelatory reverb.

What wants to be revealed right now, and how can I ready myself for whatever's brought to light?

_____

_____

_____

_____

> **Tarot To-Do:** Write out a list of the twenty questions that are most meaningful to you right now. Notice which of them might be in the realm of the existentially unanswerable; which of them you've been avoiding, even though you know your soul is ready for a response; and which of them you feel must be answered by some external entity. Then, imagine tapping each on the head with a magic wand like a game show host, revealing any kind of answer that's currently available to you.

THE 2 OF SWORDS

Each tarot 2 is our custom fit for its element, descended from the intuitive hits of the Major Arcana's High Priestess card, which bears the same numeral. Here, in the slice-and-dice Swords, it represents a moment to slip on the noise-canceling headphones and bounce to the beat only you can hear. Use it to construct a protective frame around your consciousness that softens the frenzy of feedback from the sidelines and brings you face-to-face with your own evaluations of excellence.

When and why do I solicit input from those around me, and what happens when this reverb isn't available?

_____

_____

_____

_____

Tarot To-Do: Notice the feedback loops in your life, exploring when, how, and why you ask for advice or opinions from others. Get honest about how much of this input actually helps you see new perspectives and strengthens your relationships. When you solicit input from others, how much of the time are you seeking a feeling of "okayness" from outside of yourself, or trying to reconfirm something you already know to be true? Without any self-recrimination, practice plugging up some of these input valves for the day or week, seeing what kinds of intel from the self starts to rise up to the surface instead.

THE 3 OF SWORDS

The tarot's 3s all give more flesh-and-blood life to their element. But in cool, collected Air, we're asked to create a breathable balance between letting intense emotions course through us, and allowing them to "air dry" through a healthy dose of perspective. This card is here to help us siphon wisdom from strong feelings while also staying open to feeling them without shutting down completely. With the 3 of Swords firmly in hand, we balance our big old brains with our beating hearts and commit to making clear-eyed decisions in the name of our own comprehensive care.

What is my current balance between emotion and analysis, and how can I better care for myself by equilibrating this equation?

Tarot To-Do: Imagine, or actually enact, mixing up a meal made from your emotions. Choose certain spices to represent different feelings and notice the balance of flavors. Maybe a cayenne-pepper anger is dominating the entire mix. Or there's too much sweet honey hiding a more complex profile. Without shutting anything down or forcing anything forward, notice where you might adjust the levels ever so slightly to let all aspects of your being equilibrate.

THE 4 OF SWORDS

The 4s are our do-not-disturb dens, and this airy 4 is perhaps the most complete of these retreat spaces. It is here to give us permission to totally tap out, letting our minds run blank and our spirits spirit themselves away. Our automated away-message from the cosmos, whenever it arises, we're being asked to just "drop it," freezing the scene and stepping on out of it. In its vacuum seal, we learn to trust that when we're ready to come back into the office, we can slip soundlessly into the mix once again.

What needs to be dropped right now? How can I step out of the situation that I'm currently in, and how can I tend any fears about my absence from it?

_____

_____

_____

_____

Tarot To-Do: Summon whatever situation, emotion, or relationship needs absenting from right now, and picture it as a full tableau in your mind. Imagine the setting and details, as well as the moving figures within it. Now, magically stall its motion mid-stride, and take a closer look at all its constituent parts. Then, slowly remove yourself from the scene, either scrubbing yourself out with an eraser, unsticking yourself like a transferable decal, or spiriting yourself away in a swirl of stardust. How does it feel to be gone?

THE COURT CARDS

Having acclimatized to the Majors' themes and lived out the Minors' on-the-ground energies, you're now ready to try the Court Cards on for size. Let the final few weeks of the month inspire an identity exploration: using the four "styles" sketched below to see how you're channeling this card's archetype, and/or adding your own way of embodying it to the list.

The Queen of Swords: DRAW THE LINE

The tarot's quartet of Queens are our heart-shaped lockets, here to help us come closer to our innermost emotions. In October's Air element, we meet a Queen who brings both the breeze and the badass boundaries—pushing us toward clarity and asking us to slice through anything that doesn't serve the best interests of our hearts.

We might feel like building boundaries means we've got to engage in harsh exile: forcing others out and fortressing ourselves in. But this cool and clear Queen teaches us that our circles of protection can spring up from a firm love for both self and others. A line of demarcation is always a sign of respect: for our needs, and the separate space that others occupy. Sometimes, these lines might even be internal, and this Queen also invites us to explore how we can keep ourselves out of harm's way by saying "no more" to certain patterns of behavior or beliefs.

Tap this Queen by erecting your own borders—selecting one of the boundary-building styles below to help you clarify your yeses and nos.

What kind of line are you ready to draw?

_____

_____

_____

_____

_____

_____

_____

QUEEN OF SWORDS

THE TREE LINE. This style of erecting boundaries is for you if you'd like to listen more closely to your body's natural limits. You can harness it whenever you feel like you just don't have the bandwidth for something, taking a stance in the name of physical sensation. You might even voice out loud, "My body has reached its capacity," and physically retreat, closing the door and lying down.

THE HOTLINE. This style of erecting boundaries is for you if you're ready to draw the line by looking for clear answers. You can harness it whenever you want to interrupt the noise and nebulousness and take a stance for straightforwardness. Practice asking pointed questions, stating solid facts, and not being afraid to just "call it" with an unequivocal "yes" or "no."

THE LINE DANCE. This style of erecting boundaries is for you if you're ready to let your limits arise spontaneously according to the situation. You can harness it whenever you want to open to experiences without having to adopt any hard and fast stances. Explore how you might soften your preconceived notions about life just a shade, without abandoning your standards entirely.

THE LEY LINE. This style of erecting boundaries is for you if you're ready to draw more of what's important *in* instead of forcing out what's not. You can harness it whenever you want to sanctify the space around you. Start by focusing on the elements you value most—giving those people, places, and things more attention and more time, and watching the rest naturally fall away.

The Vision Board Spread

....

October's luminosity leads us from the solid ground of what's here all the way to the pink puffy clouds of what could be. Its energy ignites our desire to elevate and curate our lives according to a higher love. Use the spread below to celebrate the dual artistry of projected ideal and pure presence, uncovering beauty in both sides of the elegant equation.

Like any magic mood board, you might actually prop these cards up in a place of prominence in your space, gazing into their eyes on the daily and letting their intentions grow in the glow.

*Group 1: **The Crystal Visions.*** Consciously select three cards from the deck that you absolutely want to feel in your life. These might be energies you've already started to experience; or they could be dream queen cards that you're craving deeply, but fear will never materialize. Start by spreading them out and just feeling into their fantasia, noticing what happens to your bod and soul when you gaze upon their landscapes. If you're looking for more clarity about specific dreams or plans you have, you might identify three of these visions, and choose your cards to represent what you hope to achieve through each. For example, if one of your dreams is to become a life coach because you feel like you'll be able to affect people's lives, you might pick a card like the Emperor or the King of Wands—which carry connotations of conscious impact— to connect you with this intention.

*Group 2: **The Earth Angels.*** Now, pull three cards "blind" from the deck. These are the guides here to lead you across the floor from where you are to where you want to be. You can pull them specifically for each of the three aspirations above—selecting one each as a point A to point B instructional card; or you can summon them as more generalized energies that want to be attended to in the present so you can start moving toward your visions. Trust that their qualities want to help you cultivate more of what you'll need to achieve your dreams, without feeling like you have to strong-arm them into your strategy to meet a certain end goal.

Notice any resistance in the face of cards you'd rather not see in Group 2, and start to let your vision blur the lines between the aspirational trio and the here-today helper trio. Remember that both teams are absolutely on your side.

MAGIC TRICK:
All the Right Moves

October asks us to handcraft our own morality—divining our sense of what's good, true, and beautiful, and making bold moves accordingly. Whether we're a well-seasoned shuffler or fresh to the decks, it can sometimes be hard to trust our pulls. Are we shuffling the right way? Was that pull all wrong? By the time we've course-corrected into oblivion, we may find ourselves covered in a blanket of all seventy-eight. Take this month to notice how your hands want to shuffle and pull, letting that process be as revelatory as the cards selected. Maybe you want to fan and spread them fully on the floor, craving the expanse of an easy breezy poolside menu. Or maybe you're hard-packing and consolidating your card cuties, drawing one off the top with ceremonious certitude. Practice reading, and trusting, your process—exploring how your actual approach might illuminate your interior state.

October Tarotscopes

LIBRA: *The Queen of Swords.* On a lifelong quest to move heaven closer to earth, you show up to every situation shining a light-bright saber. October is an invite to remember that there's beauty in the battle. Back your boldest visions without backing down.

SCORPIO: *Justice.* A gut-instinct operator, your sense of rightness is best based on your inner laws. Take October to answer solely to your own reasoning. Advocate for alignment with a personalized moral code that's made entirely from the raw stuff of your very mortal coil.

SAGITTARIUS: *The Ace of Swords.* A super-fan of surprise packages, you're always ready to revel in the spontaneous. Let October remind you that the aftermath can be just as compelling as the wondering what's inside, letting revelations and realizations be reasons to rejoice.

CAPRICORN: *The Queen of Swords.* A badass boundary-keeper, you learn your own value by banking your diamonds. October is your invite to take a break from actively building the wall. Embrace the ease of just living your life without having to force the fortress into effect.

AQUARIUS: *The 3 of Swords.* The zodiac's steady-handed healer, you're here to sweep away the excess and restore things to their most vital form and function. Let October help you embrace your clear-eyed coaching capacity by using both your head and your heart to lay hands on.

PISCES: *The 2 of Swords.* The zodiac's living coral reef, you're forever ready to receive whatever fishy bits of feedback bob along. Take October to explore

what happens when you don't allow others' opinions to take up residence in your underwater home.

ARIES: *The 4 of Swords.* Born with the firm belief in your own ability to initiate, you're here to turn the entire world on with just one touch. October wants to remind you that you can create life and then let it live. Set it off and then settle into a spot where you can enjoy the show.

TAURUS: *Justice.* A please-touch pragmatist, you're adept at backing what will yield a tangible return. October encourages you to extend this capacity for instinctive moves. Let your sense of what's valuable become even stronger, and make decisions based on what just feels right.

GEMINI: *The 4 of Swords.* A street-smart learner, you power up by staying in the middle of the party mix. Take October to remember that life won't leave you behind if you step away for a second. See how facing any FOMO can actually inject your comeback with even more color.

CANCER: *The 3 of Swords.* You're a memory museum who seeks comfort in well-worn, sepia-toned sensations. October invites you to also embrace a rose-colored future. Take a no-nonsense approach to old spin cycles, and spin yourself up and away from needless hurt.

LEO: *The Ace of Swords.* When it's given freely, your glimmer and shimmer make the whole world glow. Let October inspire you to be a loving catalyst for reveals of all kinds. Spark life into showing its hand and help others surprise themselves in the process.

VIRGO: *The Empress.* With a keen eye for life's cracks and fissures, you know how to apply just the right fix. Take October to let this be an elevation of inherent beauty instead of a fault-finding exercise, drawing the best and brightest to the surface like a magic magnet.

As you leave October's land of light and prepare to meet November's night visions, begin to explore the secret worlds that pulse beneath the surfaces. Imagine all the cake layers that live under your home's foundation. Your long-lost desires tucked beneath the bed, and those urges you haven't even met yet. See how you might make more peace with all the raw materials that reside within.

Now, gather your October and November cards into two separate piles and pluck a pal from each pack. Hold up October's card to hold fast to your highest hopes, and use November's friend to courageously face a more primal part of you.

ink your teeth into your deck. Take each card's message down and into you as if your very life depended on it. You were born to brave November's beautiful beasts without turning away . . .

This month's tarot cards leave it all on the floor: *What has to die? And how will you go on?*

NOVEMBER

The Magic of the Eternal

In the Stars: November is submerged in the Fixed Water energy of Scorpio. Fixed energy amplifies, and Water energy magnetizes. In March and July, we met Water by getting carried out into Pisces' invisible currents, and then welcomed back to shore by Cancer's gestational rhythms. This month, we're ready to be drawn down toward the undersea reaches where the light of day disappears: following the potent pull of Scorpio's primal ruling planet, Pluto, in its hunt to uncover life's eternal core. A tangible way to access what Scorpio energy feels like is to explore uprooting and overturning: metal detectors bee-lining to the beauty beneath the beach; the relentlessness of a raw heart-to-heart; the composting of once-aliveness into new life. In November's glow-in-the-dark glory, our dirt and our flowers become one and the same.

In the Cards: November's cardstock is made from snakeskin and steel—each of its six archetypes a chance to both prove our till-death-do-us-part promise to partner with inevitable transformation; and a beyond-the-grave mandate to strengthen our metals that can never be melted. These cards are an exercise in facing up to the fact that everything ends. But rather than Grim Reaper mercilessness, they show us mercy itself. When we respect the actual life span of anything in our lives—be it a relationship, endeavor, or emotion—we separate what's ephemeral from what's eternal. These cards represent the deck's life/death/life cycle itself. Let them exfoliate the excess, uncover what's yours for keeps, and help you take your place among the animals: honoring the instincts within you as no different from any other foxy in this die-hard diorama.

In Your Life: To show up for November's down-and-dirty, you can play with a **daily practice** of "making peace with the primal": staying with strong urges without having to pretty them up; getting curious about deeper motivations; not shying away from or apologizing for intensity; and honestly and lovingly looking at the life spans of parts of your life. By helping us no longer fear the furriness within us, this month uncovers the forever gift of our full-range humanness—which is the only ground for lasting intimacy with self and others.

ZODIAC SIGN: Scorpio
ELEMENT: Water
QUALITY: Fixed
CARDS: Death; Judgment; the 5/6/7 of Cups; the King of Cups
MAGIC WORDS: Excavation. Mortality/Immortality. Forgiveness. Intimacy. Power.

MAJOR ARCANA

Take the first few weeks of the month to land in these card landscapes—orienting yourself to their themes and exploring their turf through meditation and visualization. You may also want to return to the inquiry questions as part of your daily practice.

Death + Judgment

November's duet of Major Arcana deities ushers us into *life's natural cycles:* feral forces here to exorcize our exoskeletons and remind us that we're made of exactly the same stuff as every other creature who roams this dirt. When we pull these cards, or choose to work with them intentionally, it's an opportunity to soften into life's organic evolutions and recognize that everything in our lives is ultimately temporary. This month, we can use these cards to support us as we embrace the end dates, and help life "go on" by contributing to our own necessary transformation. And, in the process, we can start to uncover something eternal within us that will never die.

DEATH: Season's Greetings

When we step into this card's climate, all of nature has been waiting to welcome us. The trees shiver off their leaves to pave our path. The flowers fold to make way, and the birds quiet their frenzy. A kaleidoscopic inverse of May's Empress energy, which sits on the opposite side of the astrological year, this is the stop-motion composting that will eventually beget brand-new blooms. But before the advent of new life, we're asked to let the earth slumber. The season is changing. And we are still alive, and changing, too. How could it be any different?

Despite the visceral response this card sometimes provokes with its skeleton imagery, Death doesn't signal an eerie portent of physical departure. Instead, it simply asks us to inquire into our current relationship with transformations of all kinds. Whether it's a much-desired mini shift, or a maxi movement we feel like we never would have ordered from the menu, Death reminds us that change is already a part of us on a cellular level. These bodies are always changing. Our

directions and habitats and lovers and hairstyles will all change. This is a given. In Death, we just draw to the surface what we've always known to be true: that we are no different than everything around us, and that everything ends.

Whenever we work with this card, we're invited to explore what's most natural in this moment and what posture we could adopt to honor our life's shifts and shimmies. This might be hard to divine at first, as all sorts of big feels can bust out in the face of transformation. But on a bone-deep level, some part of us already knows how to change. How will we slough off our snakeskin? Sometimes, we'll hold fast and fierce against the tornados of change—clinging to the tree with gritted teeth before we're ultimately torn from it. Sometimes, we'll want to celebrate our phoenix-like parties: flinging our old selves off the high-dive and straight onto life's pyre. Other times, we might slip along the River Styx like a mist, letting transformation feel quiet and almost imperceptible. Just like nature itself, there are a million ways to morph.

At the heart of this card beats November's most daring demand: **to meet both the ephemeral and the eternal**. Each time we arrive in Death, we're asked to stand before ourselves with an unwavering gaze, reading the map of life that lives in our skin. It's all there: all that's been lived, loved, and lost; and all that's ours for life. We'll have our notions about what will stick around and endure, meant for the long haul. But Death might have other plans. And when we turn toward it instead of away, it shows us that we can become a precious part of this process of change: no longer feeling powerless in the face of the temporary, but empowered to face the seasons of our lives for however long they last.

 TURF TIP Explore Death through landscapes that reckon with endings while remaining regenerative. Think compost sites, ancient ruins, vigils, and death cafés.

ASK YOURSELF:

What "season" of life am I in right now—spring, summer, fall, winter?

How can I meet more of myself there?

What is changing in my life right now, and how do I feel about it?

How can I honor these shifts? And how can I handle the grief that might arise?

Where does the ephemeral live within me? And what is eternal within me?

_____

_____

_____

_____

_____

_____

_____

_____

_____

_____

_____

_____

_____

_____

_____

_____

_____

_____

JUDGMENT: Mighty Mercy

When we step into this card's climate, we might not even notice the shift at first. A slow-building, epic energy of evolution, whenever we work with this card, the plate tectonics of our lives are at play on some level. As the world turns on its axis, we can imagine Judgment's offerings as a eulogy that happens while we're still alive. And as we listen in to the story of our life so far, we begin to find it in our hearts to settle our scores, forgive ourselves and others, and get on with living out the rest of our time on this planet in the style that's most meant for us, no matter what.

In some ways, this is a graduate-level course in the forces that fire through the Mars-ruled Tower card. Judgment is ruled by Mars' larger-scale parent planet, Pluto. After the Tower helped us explore the creative tension between us making moves versus getting moved, Judgment asks us to soften this struggle and participate in an even grander evolutionary plan. We can start to do this by noticing the magnetics of our lives: what naturally pulls us closer and pushes us away, and how we handle those insistences. We might begin by examining the things we keep wanting and not getting. Or the things we keep wanting, but which feel godawful to get. Whatever our primal patterns, Judgment asks us to extend our acceptance toward them—allowing for the possibility that maybe, there are some things we won't ever escape from or "fix" in this lifetime. When we stop trying to forcibly purge stuck patterning, we can start to open to inevitable evolution that happens all on its own—**finding forgiveness, and humanizing ourselves into another scale of power entirely**.

We sometimes think that forgiveness means giving up or giving in; that our ability to hold ourselves and others accountable for actions protects our willpower, and that releasing these evaluative measures will render us spineless blobs. But Judgment tells us a different story. When we find forgiveness, says this card, we actually grow much, much larger—wide enough to hold the whole of our humanity therein. Rather than pushed-down powerlessness or blobby blamelessness, fierce forgiveness expands our life landscape. When we consciously choose to commune with this card, we find that our power doesn't come from our defense against powerlessness, but from our omnivorousness—our ability to take it all in. When we open up to this epic scale of existence, it turns our molehill battles into mountainous majesty.

It can sometimes be hard to know what exactly to "do" with this card, and the way of being that it offers is best found in the grandstands of nature itself: inviting us to make like the Grand Canyon or the Northern Lights by connecting to power sources that gain their force by having been shaped by even bigger forces. A lifetime achievement award in the art of acceptance, the more we rise to meet this card's call, the mightier our lives will become.

 TURF TIP Explore Judgment through landscapes of epic wonder that answer to their own evolutionary calls. Think volcanic islands, fault lines, energy vortexes, and mega stadiums.

What am I trying to change right now that I know, on some level, may not ever change? And what inevitable changes do I know I'm being called to make?

What's asking for my forgiveness and acceptance?

If I were to eulogize my life in this moment, what would I say about my time on earth, and how might this reckoning inspire me to live the rest of my life differently?

What is my personal definition of power, and how and when do I feel most connected to it within me?

_____

_____

_____

_____

_____

_____

_____

_____

_____

_____

_____

_____

_____

_____

_____

_____

_____

_____

THE MINOR ARCANA

After exploring the big old biospheres of the Majors, you're ready to get nitty-gritty with the on-the-ground teachings of the Minors. Let the next few weeks of the month feel like a living laboratory as you practice responding to these cards by taking direct action and noticing how they show up in your everyday life.

The 5, 6, and 7 of Cups:
THE HEART WILL GO ON

Death and Judgment ask us to powerfully participate in inevitable evolutions by accepting life's end dates and primal pulls. While you watch it all transform before your very eyes, this trio of Minor Arcana cards can become *your private karaoke room*. Each card is an accompaniment to life's longings, loves, losses, and learning-to-love-all-over-agains. They're here to keep the beat and the melody of your heart soaring through both the swan songs and the rebirth power ballads.

THE 5 OF CUPS

Despite their rep for poking and prodding at our softest parts, the 5s never mean any harm—they're here to give us a good soul workout and build muscle that matters. In the sepia-toned Cups, we're invited to explore our heart's absences. While this doesn't have to signal the searing grief of an epic loss, its energy is always a reminder that we can bring our presence to whatever feels gone. We can use this card to help us show up to tend the hollows within us that have been left by departures of all kinds.

What is gone from my life right now, and how might I acknowledge this absence?

_____

_____

_____

_____

_____

_____

_____

_____

_____

_____

Tarot To-Do: We've all got little cemeteries within us where the faithful departed reside. Begin to investigate these hallowed grounds by gently exploring some of the partings within you. Maybe it's a project that you poured your whole heart into but never really kissed goodbye. Or it's a part of your spirit that's no longer with you in the same way it once was. With incredible softness for yourself, take a tour through some of these hollows—visiting each grave in your mind's eye and saying an adieu.

THE 6 OF CUPS

Each 6 is a fully inflated pool float, here to cushion and carry us back into the flow of life. Complete with beverage holder and head pillow, in the Cups suit, this card gifts us the courage to come back to love. Akin to the day when a fever finally breaks or a breakup stops being the first, last, and only thought on our minds, this card wants to recolor the world gone gray and return us to our resilient, sweet selves, who've been with us through it all. It reminds us that whatever our heartache histories, our hearts can, and will, and *must* go on.

How does my heart stage its comebacks, renewing and returning after periods of shutdown? What have I always loved, no matter what?

_____
_____
_____
_____
_____
_____
_____
_____
_____
_____

Tarot To-Do: Taking stock of your heart season right now, explore the resources you'd need most to stage a comeback, either tapping them in real-time if you feel a rebirth coming on, or readying them to be at your disposal for a future return. These could be songs, textures, connections to friends, comfort foods—whatever tried-and-trues best bring you back to life after a period of dormancy, assuring you that loving, again and again, can absolutely be accomplished.

THE 7 OF CUPS

Each tarot 7 is a call to mature our relationship to its element and create our own set of standards. Here, in the Cups suit, we're asked to let our heart want more of what it wants. While there are certainly times when we're asked to interrogate our desires and decide whether or not they're "good" for us, the 7 of Cups wants us to challenge the notion of good versus bad. Instead, this 7 beckons us to just go ahead and want, no matter where it leads—letting our urges remind us that there are as many modes of loving and lusting after as there are lovers alive.

Which of my desires am I evaluating on a good/bad binary, and why? How can I learn to better love my own longings?

_____

_____

_____

_____

_____

_____

_____

_____

Tarot To-Do: Map your desire-appetites through time, exploring how what's magnetized you has evolved through different life moments. This can be connected to partnership, such as how your "type" of friends and lovers has shifted over the years. But you can also include all kinds of desire maps—from changing favorite foods, to styles of music and art. Let the experience feel playfully adolescent and maybe even a little bit obsessive, as you assess your history and assert your right to love whatever you're currently craving.

THE COURT CARDS

Having acclimatized to the Majors' themes and lived out the Minors' on-the-ground energies you're now ready to try the Court Cards on for size. Let the final few weeks of the month inspire an identity exploration: using the four "styles" sketched below to see how you're channeling this card's archetype, and/or adding your own way of embodying it to the list.

The King of Cups: HEAL YOUR HUMANNESS

The tarot's Kings are always calls to make a home on life's range—allowing our acceptance of a wider width to become our power source. Here, in the Water element, we're asked to expand our emotional range: holding more of our human experience without holding back, and humanizing ourselves more in the process.

We can look to this King whenever we're overwhelmed by ginormous emotions; in search of greater empathy for self or others; or longing to connect with our identity as a powerful healing presence here on earth. When we slip into its therapeutic tub, we increase our capacity to abide and stay with, no matter the water temperature. With this card's help, we no longer have to try to fix any feelings we don't fancy, and can swap our constrictive fishbowls of sensation for the whole of the emotion ocean.

Tap this King to step into your rightful role as a majestic holder of the whole human heart. Select the healing figure below that most appeals, and use it to inspire your own ability to welcome whatever feelings come up.

How can you become more human?

_____

_____

_____

_____

_____

KING OF CUPS

THE DEPTH THERAPIST. This approach to welcoming humanness invites you to spelunk below the surface and excavate unconscious treasure. Connect with this healing style if you're ready to awaken curiosity about the whole of the human experience. Let inquiries into hidden motivations and the source of behavioral patterns help you make peace with all the ways in which people can be people.

THE CELESTIAL SURGEON. This approach to welcoming humanness invites you to lay hands directly on any big feels and pragmatically approach life's primal parts. Connect with this healing style if you're ready to lean into the visceral expression of emotions. Remind yourself that we're all "just animals" with felt-sense feedback loops and assess what needs tending without judgment.

THE ENERGY HEALER. This approach to welcoming humanness invites you to adopt a more remote touch as you touch in with feelings. Connect with this healing style if you're ready to channel a spacious, meditative "just happening" stance. Watch sensations rise and fall, continue to live through them all, and picture all of us people as part of a breathing patchwork of pulsations.

THE LIFE COACH. This approach to welcoming humanness invites you to become a compassion champion who rallies the best of humanity through direct reinforcement. Practice encouraging supportive choices for yourself and others without chastising or correcting past missteps.

The Beauty in the Beasts Spread

An extension of October's call to clarify our own definitions of right and wrong, November asks us to investigate the lines we draw between "good" and "bad." This spread can be perfect for moments when you feel internally split—suppressing or pushing away some aspect of a situation. Know that you can tread lightly through this spread, working with one "beasty" at a time.

*Group 1: **The Beasty Feasts.*** Start by taking the cards out of the deck that activate you in some way—make you nervous, make your heart sink, or just feel plain old "ick." Place them in a pile, settle your system, shuffle them up, and pluck four cards, one for each of the transformational roles below, all animal symbols for this month's Scorpio spirit.

*Card 1: **The Scorpion.*** This card invites you to bear its surface sting, as best you're able, letting this puncture become a portal by noticing what happens in your system after the initial ick. Just sit with it for a sweet moment and see what starts to emerge under the pain point.

*Card 2: **The Snake.*** This card invites you to get low with it, bending to embrace its energy as part of the human experience, and letting its natural course pave a pathway toward making peace with your primalness. Notice how you can start to slither along in its style for even a second.

*Card 3: **The Eagle.*** This card invites you to elevate your perspective on it, noticing what you might be missing when you get mired in one meaning of it, and opening up to its purpose in a larger plan. Imagine looking back on it from another point in your life and seeing where its magic might land.

*Card 4: **The Phoenix.*** This card invites you to transform it into a power creature, allowing whatever intense feelings you harbor toward it to live fully and even grow larger. Explore how these emotions might actually fuel you, opening up to strength that's tapped when you don't turn away.

*Group 2: **The Beauty Bites.*** Now, draw four cards from the remaining crew that you left in the deck, which don't feel as confronting. You can think of these as your headlamps—here to help you navigate the darkrooms of Group 1.

MAGIC TRICK:
Building Intimacy

November encourages us to investigate what's below the surface and under the bed, and to come into deeper intimacy with a fuller range of feelings. Take time this month to bond with your deck like a beloved, sharing more of yourself with it. Begin by noticing how you might get dolled up for card pulls, always turning them over in a serene state surrounded by candles, or after you've stilled your mind. See how it might feel to instead pull in rawer states, experimenting with shuffles from a work bathroom stall, on a cacophonous street corner, or before you've brushed your teeth. While you're at it, explore how you can better believe what your deck shows you, trusting both your own hands and the archetypes that have emerged, even when they might initially feel icky. And don't be afraid to get a little obsessive and intense with your new love—perhaps even planning a weekend where you don't leave your deck's side, staring into each card's life-world until you don't have eyes for anything else.

November Tarotscopes

SCORPIO: *The King of Cups.* Amid all your survivalist resilience, you sometimes lose sight of the tender process of living life. Take November to relish your role as a humanizer. Extending compassion to the hearts around you can be your most courageous act yet.

SAGITTARIUS: *The 7 of Cups.* Back to the buffet for thirds and fourths, one of your main missions is to make love to life's more-ness. Take November to dive deep into each desire without holding anything in reserve or even having to assess what purpose your "wants" serve.

CAPRICORN: *Judgment.* The timelines of existence are tattooed on your heart. But rather than seeing them as cause for doom, let November remind you that your wisdom is here to humanize you, helping you find forgiveness while you're still here.

AQUARIUS: *The 6 of Cups.* Your spirit relishes rebirths of all kinds. November is a call to explore your more private, phoenix-like transformations. Let yourself remember that change isn't just about composting but about coming *back* to life, and relish a sweet rise from the ashes.

PISCES: *Death.* A lover here to loosen life's grip, you're able to embrace ever-changing evanescence more than most. Take November to harness a fiercer flavor of transformation. Become death itself: reveling in your right to consciously toss ancient matter on the pyre.

ARIES: *The 6 of Cups.* One of your greatest strengths is your whack-a-mole ability to keep on coming back for more even when life smacks you down. Let November remind you that popping up again doesn't have to be a power struggle. Take pure pleasure in your comebacks.

 **TAURUS:** *Death.* The sign energy that courses closest to nature itself, you know you're no different than the dirt and the flowers. Let November be an invite to show up through periods of both blooming and composting. Whatever the season, use its treasures to forge an unshakeable trust in your life cycles.

 **GEMINI:** *The 5 of Cups.* A honeycomb of a human, you sensitively keep watch over all of life's crossroads and portals. November invites you to fully embrace your role as a channel for transformation. Walk yourself and others through changes with the power of your courageous presence.

 **CANCER:** *The King of Cups.* Embracing every feeling in the emotion ocean, you help give the whole human experience a wider home. Let November help you revel in this role. Listen and let without assessment, and make your cove of compassion even more capacious.

 LEO: *The 5 of Cups.* Your eternal summer spirit glows on and on without dimming. November reminds you to bring your solar-powered presence forward during moments that feel empty of light. Let your purpose be to show up on the side of life, still warm, even when things grow cold.

 VIRGO: *The 7 of Cups.* A participant in the primal symphony of life here on earth, you understand the range of human appetite. Take November to drop any analysis and get curious about all these possible cravings—embracing the multitude of impulses that present.

 **LIBRA:** *Judgment.* With a keen sense of right and wrong, you can sometimes hold yourself to task for perceived missteps. Let November be a reprieve from any self-inflicted harshness about your actions. Let yourself be "just a human" and handle it all the best way you know how.

As you jump from November's jungle gym of animal instinct into December's roulette wheel of road readiness, explore how things get rocked and rolled. A kid somersaulting down a hill. A jet plane barreling across the runway toward its exuberant ascent. Notice how everything alive gets made into something more through momentum.

Now, gather your November and December cards into two separate piles and pluck a pal from each pack. Secure whatever is eternal with your November card, and use December's card to help you break out the bubbly and celebrate this unbreakable bit.

Shuffle your deck and place your bets. As your year closes, December's confetti-covered tarmac wants to ride you farther, faster, and ever onward. So climb aboard . . .

This month's tarot cards come with wheels up and wings spread: *Go ahead and toss them to the winds. Because you can handle whatever hand gets dealt.*

DECEMBER

The Magic of Wildness

In the Stars: December courses with the Mutable Fire energy of Sagittarius. In April and August, we met Fire through the on switch of Aries' instigation, and the warm glow of Leo's passion play. Now, at the close of the calendar year, we finish our spin through the element of immortality at the biggest, boldest barbecue of them all. Plumped up by the faith-building fatness of ruling planet Jupiter, December's grand finale wants us to roll the top down and risk it all. Because life is worth so much more than its opposite. A tangible way to access Sagittarius energy is to watch things adventuring: losing sight of a stranger's quick turns down a street; vines spilling straight over the side of the pot; a wild night out that sprawls before you. Everything around us is having a go at it and taking a chance, as we head off to parts unknown in search of something.

In the Cards: December's cardstock is made from road-ready, supersized stuff, and each of its six archetypes is an invite to shake out our manes, stretch our mile-high stems, and keep coming back for more. With a rep for being "lucky," Sagittarius' fortune isn't about some inborn golden status, but instead about rolling the dice born from the bold belief—even, and especially, when the whole deck seems to be stacked against us—that our own existence is ultimately on our side. Rather than a naïve optimism that denies difficulties, these cards want us to develop a hearty lust for living—using all available ingredients that come our way as more fuel for the endless adventure. Let them take you absolutely anywhere, on a wing and a prayer.

In Your Life: To hit December's open-road, you can embrace a **daily practice** of "seeking more life": letting this calendar culmination be a celebration that both commemorates all that's gone down, but also keeps the party going as you plan your future fests; searching for "signs" of your life's megawatt meaning and purpose; building your tolerance for risk and releasing control; exploring what stokes your faith and how you communicate with your personal form of divinity; and setting off in search of whatever gets your blood pumping, wherever it may lead.

ZODIAC SIGN: Sagittarius
ELEMENT: Fire
QUALITY: Mutable
CARDS: the Wheel of Fortune; Temperance; the 8/9/10 of Wands; the Knight of Wands
MAGIC WORDS: Risk. Co-creation. Faith. Adventure. Celebration.

MAJOR ARCANA

Take the first few weeks of the month to land in these card landscapes—orienting yourself to their themes and exploring their turf through meditation and visualization. You may also want to return to the inquiry questions as part of your daily practice.

The Wheel of Fortune + Temperance

December's pair of Major Arcana deities gives us our *tickets to ride:* faith-fortifying, all-access passes to the roads that naturally rise to meet us whenever we fully commit to climbing aboard. When we pull these cards, or choose to work with them intentionally, it's a chance to throw our hands in the air and wave them like we absolutely care. They're about uncovering our beliefs in the workings of the Universe; discovering the larger-than-life significance of our own existence; and loosening our grip and letting whatever form of divinity we believe in take the wheel. These cards ask us to summon trust that somehow, it will all work out, in the end.

THE WHEEL OF FORTUNE: As the World Turns

Stepping into this card's climate happens when we switch on cruise control, prop our feet on the dash, and settle in to enjoy the view. Back at the fortune-telling tent, something is cooking. Cards are getting shuffled. Hands are getting dealt. But we no longer need to peep behind the curtains through frightened fingers as we await our fate. Instead, we're content to keep on living as the wheels turn, while the surprise card party unfolds of its own accord.

Whenever we work with this card, we're asked to explore how to relax more fully into life's twists and turns. Infused with a "pay our money and take our chances" form of freedom, the Wheel asks us to let more of our lives Tilt-A-Whirl on autopilot, as we revel in whatever the ride with our high spirits still intact. There will certainly be life moments when we get dealt hands we neither want nor deserve. But with the Wheel's help, we can start to move beyond our fear about good/bad fates. When we interrupt our control over what life is sending us and just **show up for this mini moment with a willingness to take a spin**, we can let each life happening have

WHEEL OF FORTUNE

its very own adventure. When left to its own devices, even the sticky stuff in our lives may surprise us by setting off chain reactions in a much grander plan. Tucked into our Ferris wheel basket, not yet able to glimpse the big-picture view from the top, we're whisked toward the more, and even better, that's to come.

Adopting this carnival-ride consciousness calls us to consider who or what we think controls the trajectory of our lives. How do we respond when life appears to take us somewhere we don't understand, or haven't planned for? Sometimes, we're stuck watching from the sidelines, reluctant to get swept away in forward motion. But the Wheel reminds us that it is always turning. And co-creation can begin when we stop trying to figure out who's driving or where exactly we're headed, and just join the celebratory conga line of top-down convertibles.

Whether or not we can see it, our life is always heading off in search of new life—be it percolating beneath the surface, or barreling down the runway at breakneck speed. Wiling out with this card means learning to establish greater trust in both the visible and invisible motions that are always leading somewhere, even when we can't see or control the destination. From this down-to-head-anywhere place of presence, we start to travel hand in hand with destiny—letting a deeper kinship with our life path spring directly from our capacity to join the party and pop off in whatever direction the night takes.

 TURF TIP Explore the Wheel of Fortune through landscapes where adventurous motion leads to unexpected ends. Think amusement parks, spontaneous weekend getaways, surprise parties, and casino floors.

ASK YOURSELF:

What kind of trajectory is unfolding in my life right now?

Is it a moment where I see the path clearly, or is the road obscured?

How can I settle in to better enjoy the ride either way?

Where do I feel like I'm heading, and who or what do I believe is deciding the course of my life right now?

Where am I on the continuum of hands-off versus hands-on control?

How can I place a bit more of my life on autopilot?

How might I summon more faith in life's twists and turns?

_____

_____

_____

_____

_____

_____

_____

_____

_____

_____

_____

_____

_____

_____

TEMPERANCE: The Meaning of Life

Stepping into this card's climate often occurs at a bend in the road. We may feel like we've lost our way just a bit, caught at some kind of what-does-it-all-mean crossroads and searching for any kind of headlights to point us in the right direction. Or we've already started to glimpse a glimmer of light through the darkness, exhilarated by the belief that our little life is so much more than "just this." Wherever we are, Temperance wants to meet, match, and magnify us. Its energy beckons us to ask life our biggest and boldest questions, and to live out the answers that hold the most meaning for us.

Like all Fire-sign energy, which also injects April and August with its vigor and verve, Sagittarius-ruled December is concerned with both the exhilaration of life as we know it and the larger-than-life meanings we mythically infuse into it. And nowhere in the whole of the deck does life get more amped up and tricked out than in the blazing glory of Temperance. Whenever we work with this card, **we set off in search of significance**, seeking the through lines and theme songs that reoccur throughout our lives.

Each of us makes meaning in a different way, and Temperance invites us to consider the unique credos and mission statements that make our lives worth living. Some of us are scientists, relishing facts and proofs. For others, meaning comes in streaks of color or sound or scent, all of life a sensational sweep that's meant to be enjoyed rather than questioned. Still others are head-over-heels romantics, craving a place in the center of a story with dramatic turns and roller-coaster highs and lows. Whatever our drama, Temperance wants us to live in complete accordance with its mandate. It asks us to accept our mission as meaning-makers of our own lives.

This card's visual iconography often features an emboldened angel with wings spread wide, and when we partner with Temperance, we're asked to open up to the presence of whatever our conception of the divine might be. If the Wheel of Fortune invited us to start dancing with destiny, Temperance asks us to summon an even fuller faith in a form of fate that's actively co-created rather than fixed or force-fed to us. When we commit body and soul to whatever has the most meaning for us, we start to find that we naturally see signs of this story everywhere. And when we see these correspondences, the invisible powers that be get inspired to co-write even more of that tale with us, sending us little signals and poetic pieces to affirm our own sense of our lives.

Whether ours is a love story, a detective tale, or a life of the mind, Temperance wants to help us pen it. By committing to our belief in something bigger, we give life the best of us, and it can give back in turn: interceding on our behalf because it actually knows what we're "all about." Temperance lights up our all-night roadside shrine and teaches us to pray at whatever our altar might be. Because when we take even one baby step in the direction of our destiny, the divine within us, and all around us, intervenes.

 TURF TIP Explore Temperance through landscapes where meaning is made co-creatively. Think public art installations and immersive theater, roadside shrines, choose-your-own adventures, and whatever spaces hold the most significance for *you*.

ASK YOURSELF:

How do I make meaning out of my life experiences, especially in moments that appear to be utterly devoid of it?

What themes and patterns have I sensed in my life, and how do I feel about them?

If I had to categorize my life as a genre, what would I call it?

What are my beliefs about the Universe at large?

What are my feelings about fate and my own co-creative role within it?

How do I communicate and commune with my form of "spirit" or the "divine"?

_____

_____

_____

_____

_____

_____

_____

_____

_____

_____

_____

_____

_____

THE MINOR ARCANA

After exploring the big old biospheres of the Majors, you're ready to get nitty-gritty with the on-the-ground teachings of the Minors. Let the next few weeks of the month feel like a living laboratory, as you practice responding to these cards by taking direct action, and noticing how they show up in your everyday life.

The 8, 9, and 10 of Wands:
GOING THE DISTANCE

As we let the Wheel of Fortune and Temperance take us off-road in search of December's rise-to-meet-us wildness, we can look to this trio of Minor Arcana kiddies to fuel our tanks and keep them running for the long haul. You can think of this triplet as *your roadside assistance*. Each card is a pitstop partner for embracing the twists and turns, reading the signs, enjoying the sights, and maintaining a comfy cruising speed without overheating.

THE 8 OF WANDS

All 8s in the tarot bring us closer to their elements, asking us to undress our resistance and see what gets revealed. Here in the fiery Wands, we limber up by learning to read and respond to the symbols that surround us all the time. As you work with the 8 of Wands, notice what's coming "at" you, and pay special attention to whatever synchronicities might be playing out before your eyes. Expanding your capacity to notice and interpret them gives you the ability to divine meaning from the scavenger hunt that is your life.

What signs is my own life showing me right now, and what do they mean?

_____

_____

_____

_____

_____

_____

_____

_____

Tarot To-Do: Imagine that your entire environment was a tarot deck, and practice psychically reading the cards that come calling. Notice the numbers on a clock when you get an important call. The glimmer in the eye of someone you meet for the first time, who could be a future beloved. Overheard music at stoplights and strangers' conversations drifting through the air. Without reaching too strenuously or forcing connections, play with the meaning of all these magic moments. By day's end, write out a phrase that sums up the theme of these messages, and explore how you might respond.

THE 9 OF WANDS

A private greenroom of its element, each tarot 9 offers us an opportunity to take a personalized pause and gather ourselves in solitude. In the Wands, this marks the locker room life-force moment where we take a mini break from go-hard-or-go-home living. It reminds us that we're in life for the long haul, and taking a temporary bench seat doesn't have to derail our momentum. If we want to keep on giving our endeavors the best of us, we've got to make like any good coach: managing our energy levels, refueling when necessary, and giving ourselves the ultimate pep talk when it's time to get back in the game.

How do I manage my energy levels? What depletes and restores them?

_____

_____

_____

_____

_____

_____

_____

_____

_____

_____

_____

_____

Tarot To-Do: As you go about your day, picture your energy level like a character's health meter in a video game. Notice what people, situations, and emotional experiences seem to take away from and deplete it, and which supercharge you with more lives. You might even give yourself a finite number of energetic units, and when you get to the end of them, just forcibly insert a pause until you've powered up once again.

THE 10 OF WANDS

Every tarot 10 is a celebration of all the treats that have come before. In the Wands suit, we're here to feast on the range of wins and losses we've lived through, and to embrace the notion that our personal mojo is just one piece in a much larger power dynamic where each of us participates at our own level. Working with it asks us to simultaneously acknowledge our capacities for courage and our human limits. When we recognize both, we can better understand exactly the kinds of heroes we were born to be, and the missions that are made to best match us.

What are my personal definitions of winning and losing? Which battles are mine to fight, and how can I embrace more of my mission by dropping the struggles that aren't meant for me?

_____

_____

_____

_____

_____

_____

_____

_____

_____

Tarot To-Do: Sketch out a full portrait of all the battles you're engaged in right now, however big or small. Imagine yourself superhero-suiting yourself up for each of them and running into the fray head-on. As you play out each of these scenarios in your head, notice which feel like losing struggles that aren't really yours, and which feel more aligned with a deeper sense of your authentic mission. Now, for the battles that aren't yours, freeze the frame and pop some other being or force into place to continue to fight those out for you, refocusing your own life-force on the capes that best fit you.

THE COURT CARDS

Having acclimatized to the Majors' themes, and lived out the Minors' on-the-ground energies, you're now ready to try the Court Cards on for size. Let the final few weeks of the month inspire an identity exploration: using the four "styles" sketched below to see how you're channeling this card's archetype, and/or adding your own way of embodying it to the list.

The Knight of Wands: TAKE A CHANCE

The Knights are our Soul Train sidekicks, here to cheer us on from the sidelines as we shimmy to life's shifting rhythms. Here, in December's Sagittarius-ruled energy, we're learning to throw down the gauntlet—so secure in our self-expression that we can open up to improv mode and spontaneously rise to meet whatever challenges come hurling back at us.

The ability to take risks means we need to have faith in our internal strength. This Knight reminds us that whenever we take a chance, we back ourselves in the belief that we'll be able to handle whatever the consequences. And by building more risk tolerance in a life that's always part lottery, we open ourselves up to more luck—increasing our odds each time we're willing to throw down.

Tap this Knight by placing your bets and gambling on yourself this month. Peruse the adventure styles below and see which you might want to take for a spin.

What am I ready to risk?

_____

_____

_____

_____

_____

_____

_____

_____

KNIGHT OF WANDS

THE HIGH-ROLLER. This risk-taking approach is for you if you're ready to adopt an all-or-nothing attitude—giving it all you've got and seeing what you get. Practice committing fully to a course of action and seeing it through to the end, no matter the result. As you reach the end of whatever your endeavor, let both the wins and losses remind you that you're alive and that you tried.

THE CARD SHARK. This risk-taking approach is for you if you're ready for a slightly more measured approach: capitalizing on your capacity to read the room before you place your bets. Practice taking a chance based on the wisdom of past experience and sheer instinct. Let yourself size up the situation in a second, and then make a move in accordance with your intuition.

THE SLOT MACHINE. This risk-taking approach is for you if you're ready to play with leaving life entirely up to chance: pulling the lever and seeing what cherries pop up. Practice dropping all decision-making and strategy with regard to a life situation, even for a second. Witness whatever arises and then go ahead and just give it another spin.

THE SCRATCH TICKET. This risk-taking approach is for you if you're ready to touch in with tinier tastes of the untamable before you commit to gambling it all away. Practice opening up to low-stakes spontaneity: for example, not having to choose where you go for dinner, or have the last word in a conversation. Let each life moment feel like a chance for a mini adventure.

The Choose-Your-Own Adventure Spread

....

December invites us to spread our tendrils across life's highways and byways, exploring adventurous alternatives to the straight and narrow with an up-to-be-surprised spirit. You can use the spread below to start stretching your longest legs and stoking your strength for spontaneous quests.

Give yourself multiple routes through the archetypes, pulling at least three cards for each category below and lining them up as three or more possible journeys through the prompts. Then, let yourself pick whichever quartet of cards feels like the most compelling course and hit the road.

If you've been traveling through this book chronologically, you might harness this spread as a special moment to close out the calendar and kick off your year to come—choosing the adventure that gets you extra jazzed to journey ever onward.

Card 1 (x 3): **The Hero.** This card represents the part of you that's being asked to step up and step forward to start a new adventure. Summon its qualities to send yourself off in wild style, imagining that you're fully clothed in its bodysuit as an inherent part of your being.

Card 2 (x 3): **The Sidekick.** This card represents the snuggle bug who wants to walk alongside you—providing extra padding, supplemental skills, and a healthy dose of humor. Embrace it as an add-on that's always on hand to be tapped during tapped-out moments.

Card 3 (x 3): **The Mission.** This card represents the big old what's-it-all-worth theme that you're working, here to keep you honest about what you came to live through and learn. Conjure its credo to stay the course and commit to questing after its highest octave of expression.

Card 4 (x 3): **The Magic Key.** This card represents the secret delights and unexpected treasures that you're invited to uncover throughout your adventure. Look out for signs of this archetype along your way, and stay open to being surprised by how its energy might manifest.

* ✸ *

MAGIC TRICK:
Street Signs

December is made for embracing on-the-ground, experiential learning. Take time this month to put all of your esoteric knowledge to use in the real world by going on a treasure hunt for all seventy-eight tarot archetypes in your everyday life. You might start by looking for literal symbols: a Strength-looking lion at your neighbor's front gate; two cups atop a fancy café table. Then, start to build into increasing abstraction, noticing when you encounter the feeling of these energies and calling them by their new tarot names. Maybe you accept a promotion at work and feel tenderly Chariot-like about this graduation of spirit. Or you watch a baby having a tantrum and catch a whiff of 5 of Wands' have-it-out-with-self heat. Start to document these living symbols as they live for you, snapping a pic or jotting them down as you begin to build your own breathable sense of each card's truest meaning.

· →→ 👁 ←← ·

December Tarotscopes

SAGITTARIUS: *Temperance.* Here to earn all the Universe's honorary doctorates, you're on a quest for the truthiest truth at every turn. Take December to tap the credos that have stayed the course, committing to whatever's held the most meaning for you through thick and thin.

CAPRICORN: *The Knight of Wands.* The zodiac's greatest weatherizer, you've got the apocalypse cellar stocked. Take December to trust that you have all the canned green beans you'll ever need, and open up to the improv adventures that don't need any anticipating.

AQUARIUS: *The 10 of Wands.* Ready to serve the whole of humanity, you often end up with your arms stuffed with passion projects. Take December to toss a few in the air, and see what surprising insights about your core mission can come from lightening your load.

PISCES: *The 9 of Wands.* A watery spirit lifter whispering affirmations from the wings, you're comfy keeping all beings buoyant. Take December to embrace your status as your own personal life coach. Instead of only focusing on others, power yourself up for the next round.

ARIES: *The 10 of Wands.* You're a caped wonderkid who can make a mission out of even the most miniscule issues. Take December to treat your ready-for-battle status as a precious resource to be directed at only the worthiest targets. Drop extra superhero suits at the cleaners in favor of those that fit like a glove.

TAURUS: *The Wheel of Fortune.* While you have a rep for being change-averse, any tendency to get stuck stems from your penchant for steeping yourself in

sweet sensation. Take December to pad yourself up in the pleasures of the present so that you don't even notice the road's turns.

GEMINI: *The 8 of Wands.* As the mail service that delivers messages through the cosmos, you're poised to carry notes from Source at any moment. Let December remind you that even the smallest signs are meant for you. Pick up on intuitive intel and respond accordingly.

CANCER: *Temperance.* You're a Cardinal Water sign kid whose mission is to follow the force of your feelings. December emboldens this birthright to go exactly where the heart leads. Refind your "why," give your rallying cry, and chart your course in accordance with your ardor.

LEO: *The Knight of Wands.* An undiluted cutie, your self-coherence is courageous. December invites you to trust so fully in your sense of self that you can spread it around. This month, risk bringing different facets of yourself forward without fearing that you'll lose the core "you."

VIRGO: *The Wheel of Fortune.* A magic maker who can find the divine in every dot, your superpower stems from shedding light on life's dazzling specks. Take December to embrace the miniature in all its majesty—focusing on the granular nature of the tasks at hand while letting the bigger adventure unfold all on its own.

LIBRA: *The 8 of Wands.* A being who knows how to weigh the options, you can find a sense of wonder in the "what-ifs." December wants you to enjoy living in these ellipses. Read the street signs of life like a treasure hunt, and choose to follow their directions wherever they might lead.

SCORPIO: *The 9 of Wands.* One of the zodiac's endurance experts, you've got staying power that makes the rest of us blush. Let December be your moment for gathering this stamina close to self, letting your reserves build slowly until they're ready to rip.

Both grand finale and eternally renewing rendezvous with your ever-changing self, the year's end is made for spreading out your entire card collection. Take your deck of seventy-eight flavors of living and place them all faceup. Then, take a look at them and imagine that they are stills from a home movie. Behold all the places you've been. Pause for a moment on each of these landscapes, calling to mind a time this year when you inhabited it. You've traveled into every shade and shape of humanness there is—the bitter, the sweet, and everything in between. You've now got everything it takes to keep on keeping on with it, whatever your hand.

Now, place your seventy-eight cards facedown and pluck one from the pack. Cross it over your heart. And let the beat go on . . .

As you wile through the twelve months of the year and forge an intimate relationship with your entire deck, you can use this index of card meanings to get a fast handle on each of the seventy-eight. These listings are bite-sized interpretations that don't cover a card's full meaning (you can find each card's thorough treatment in its corresponding month). But they can be especially handy when you feel like you're getting lost in a card or spread's complexity, and just need a quick-and-dirty to help you divine. This section can also be useful as you start to "off-road": letting the meanings in this book be a launchpad for your own intuitive interpretations of a card's greater complexity.

CARD-BY-CARD
MINI REFERENCE

THE MAJOR ARCANA
⇒ *SOUL BIOSPHERES* ⇐

These cards welcome us to explore the larger climate of our lives and
open to evolutionary change.

THE FOOL

(February). Getting good with
groundlessness, and exploring the
unknown and unknowable in any life
moment.

THE HIEROPHANT

(May). Sifting through your storehouse of embodied beliefs to examine
what you've absorbed from life, and
whether or not it still nourishes.

THE MAGICIAN

(June + September). Opening
your channel for the interception
of inspiration, and attending to
your energetic constitution as you
assimilate experiences.

THE LOVERS

(June). Communing with all the
reciprocal exchanges that want to
meet and walk with you through life.

THE HIGH PRIESTESS

(July). Heeding your private calls and
listening in to your conch shell of
intuitive wisdom.

THE CHARIOT

(July). Considering the carriers and
casings that caretake you through
graduation moments.

THE EMPRESS

(May + October). Divining your
capacity to be open to life's more-
ness, and accentuating its beauty by
placing your experiences in their best
natural light.

STRENGTH

(August). Coming forward heart-
first and letting your human touch
bring all of life closer to your arms.

THE EMPEROR

(April). Assessing your impact, and
becoming "right sized" by bearing
both your birthright to exist and the
responsibility for your existence.

THE HERMIT

(September). Going solo in some
way and honoring who you really
are when you are wholly alone.

THE WHEEL OF FORTUNE

(December). Letting things run on autopilot and developing faith in life's twists and turns instead of fearing your fate.

THE TOWER

(April). Coming alive to all the forces that want to move through you.

JUSTICE

(October). Finding the most aligned fit for you by answering to your own sense of right and wrong.

THE STAR

(February). Restoring and renewing your relationship to your original essence.

THE HANGED ONE

(March). Completing your stay in your current state, and dissolving your resistance to doing "nothing" so that something can come undone.

THE MOON

(March). Letting emotional pulls carry you into your own deep end without going under.

DEATH

(November). Turning toward seasons of change and uncovering both the ephemeral and the eternal.

THE SUN

(August). Regarding what's realest and authentically radiating your honest essence in kind.

TEMPERANCE

(December). Living in accordance with your own meaning of life and co-creating it with the help of something bigger.

JUDGMENT

(November). Funding power by finding forgiveness for your human evolutions.

THE DEVIL

(January). Sloughing off shame and unabashedly claiming inner authority.

THE WORLD

(December). Making friends with finiteness and living in line with your legacy.

THE MINOR ARCANA

⇒ *TODAY'S SPECIALS* ⇐

These cards serve us on-the-ground life leanings that inspire direct action and practical integration.

In addition to reading each specific Minor Arcana card's meaning, you can also play with combining its number and suit meanings to help you develop more personalized interpretations of the energies. For example, when you pull the 2 of Cups, you can read the entry for the "2" and the general meaning of Wands' Fire energy and then see what starts popping for you.

Aces. On-the-go essentials to help us notice where the element already exists in our environment.

2s. Personal pillars to customize our intuitive fit and direction forward in the element.

3s. Voluptuous bubbles to open us up to more of the element's flesh-and-blood humanness.

4s. Do-not-disturb hotel suites to fortify our foundations and secure us in the element.

5s. Bump and grinds to undo our grip on the element and unleash freedom through friction.

6s. Give-and-take ladles to spoon out the element's sweetness and let us love it once again.

7s. Bon voyage send-offs to coax us out of our comfort zones and into greater maturity within the element.

8s. Soft brushes to comb us closer to the element and render us more responsive and available.

9s. Private treehouses to help us process our experience of the element and bring us back to self.

10s. Full-spread buffet tables where we feast on our entire journey through the element.

THE WANDS
FIRE ELEMENT

Aliveness, self-expression, and larger-than-life meaning making.

ACE OF WANDS (April). Stoking the next spark by turning toward what's turning on.

2 OF WANDS (April). Relishing your right to rub two sticks together and make something happen.

3 OF WANDS (April). Becoming a baby bud beginner who finds boldness in the not-yet-knowing-how.

4 OF WANDS (April). Throwing yourself a power party to enjoy the impact of your already-good-enough efforts.

5 OF WANDS (August). Becoming a true-blue friend to self and sticking by your own side through inner strife.

6 OF WANDS (August). Beholding the epicness of your very own existence.

7 OF WANDS (August). Trusting that no one else can give exactly what you've got.

8 OF WANDS (December). Reading the signs that life throws at you and imbuing them with intuitive meaning.

9 OF WANDS (December). Assessing and tending your energy levels for the precious long haul.

10 OF WANDS (December). Uncovering more of your mission by resting from the battles that aren't yours to fight.

THE PENTACLES
⇒ *EARTH ELEMENT* ⇐

Embodiment, tangible resources, and ritualized rhythms.

ACE OF PENTACLES (January). Identifying core supports to begin your build brick by brick.

2 OF PENTACLES (January). Making room for more regalness by releasing what can't be carried.

3 OF PENTACLES (January). Relishing the rightness of your right-now role.

4 OF PENTACLES (January). Sovereignly sealing yourself into a self-sufficient structure.

5 OF PENTACLES (May). Facing fears of fallowness and forging a forever trust in fertility.

6 OF PENTACLES (May). Enjoying life's natural give-and-take without keeping score.

7 OF PENTACLES (May). Keeping your own time and stabilizing sensations of self-worth.

8 OF PENTACLES (September). Apprenticing your energy to the experience and allowing yourself to be pliably in-process.

9 OF PENTACLES (September). Taking pleasure in the particularities of your palate and serving them up on a platter.

10 OF PENTACLES (September). Soothing struggles to "have it all" by making more out of each piece that's already here.

THE SWORDS
⇒ *AIR ELEMENT* ⇐

Aspiration, reflection, and consciousness shifts.

ACE OF SWORDS (October). Invigorating your inquiries and readying for the revelations.

2 OF SWORDS (October). Cutting ties with the feedback loop and answering to self-divined standards.

3 OF SWORDS (October). Decision-making with equal parts cool head and warm heart.

4 OF SWORDS (October). Dropping out of the scene and finding serenity in blankness.

5 OF SWORDS (February). Tracking your reaction patterns and soothing what sets you off.

6 OF SWORDS (February). Re-contextualizing calcified concepts about the way things are.

7 OF SWORDS (February). Getting curious about what bobs beneath the buzz of distraction.

8 OF SWORDS (June). Reserving your right to honeycomb your way out of any dead end.

9 OF SWORDS (June). Tenderly exposing the creepy-crawlies in your consciousness.

10 OF SWORDS (June). Getting out of your head and changing your mind to match only the truthiest truths.

THE CUPS
⇒ *WATER ELEMENT* ⇐

Intimacy, fusion, and emotional pulls.

ACE OF CUPS (July). Turning on the taps of your heart and inviting your feelings to flow.

2 OF CUPS (July). Softening your self-gaze and starting to duet with the discarded parts.

3 OF CUPS (July). Welcoming honest intimacy, and real love that grows and changes.

4 OF CUPS (July). Metabolizing matters of the heart on your own tender timeline.

5 OF CUPS (November). Becoming present to the absences that have been left behind.

6 OF CUPS (November). Embracing your heart's resilience and coming back to love life again.

7 OF CUPS (November). Voraciously exploring the range of your cravings and wanting whatever you want.

8 OF CUPS (March). Eloping from a well-tread emotional pathway in your own style.

9 OF CUPS (March). Holding out your holy hope chest and hoping for the best.

10 OF CUPS (March). Savoring the singular sensation of this already-evanescing moment.

THE COURT CARDS
⇉ BODY SUITS ⇇

These cards escort us back to essential parts of our identities.

⇉ THE PAGES ⇇

Fresh-and-ready opportunities to embrace the now and re-find innocence
on the other side of experience.

PAGE OF WANDS. (April). Finding newness by exploring a fresh facet of who you are right now.

PAGE OF PENTACLES. (April). Finding newness by exploring the worldly wonders that want to awe you.

PAGE OF SWORDS. (April). Finding newness by exploring life as an ongoing learning opportunity.

PAGE OF CUPS. (April). Finding newness by exploring the imaginative force of your feelings.

Body-rocking rhythm sections here to help us take life's current currents in stride.

KNIGHT OF WANDS (December). Risking a dice roll on life and backing yourself on whatever deals get dealt.

KNIGHT OF PENTACLES (September). Bending toward your body's intelligence and using it to better take the shape of what meets you.

KNIGHT OF SWORDS (June). Lightening up to life and letting flexibility reveal new options.

KNIGHT OF CUPS (March). Finding flow by going "with" what's unfolding and getting carried.

⇒ THE QUEENS ⇐

Internal boudoirs where we tend our private essence that belongs to us alone.

QUEEN OF WANDS (April). Coming to life and reveling in your passionate presence here on the planet.

QUEEN OF PENTACLES (January). Giving yourself ground and choosing sources of support that best serve you.

QUEEN OF SWORDS (October). Protecting your borders and letting them give rise to clear sightlines.

QUEEN OF CUPS (July). Slipping away into your secret world to tend the emotional life that lives within.

Footprints of life-force where we take, make, and hold space.

KING OF WANDS (August). Generously showing up to share the gift of your presence and get back the glow that comes from giving it.

KING OF PENTACLES (May). Settling into situations and letting them take shape around you.

KING OF SWORDS (February). Widening to witness the weather patterns and let them blow through you.

KING OF CUPS (November). Healing your humanness through empathy for the emotional expanse.

INDEX

NOTES

PICTURE CREDITS

ABOUT THE
AUTHOR

Bess Matassa, PhD, is a New York–based astrology and tarot reader, teacher, and author who serves up mystical self-inquiry with a side of pop music and pasta sauce. When not busy combing the cosmos, Bess can be spotted sporting hot pink lipstick while wandering deserts and tropics. Connect @bessmatassa and bessmatassa.com.

Other titles: *The Numinous Cosmic Year: Your Astrological Almanac* (Aster, 2021); *Zodiac Signs: Leo* (Sterling, 2020); *Zodiac Signs: Virgo* (Sterling, 2020); *The Numinous Astro Deck* (Sterling, 2019).